THE SCENE / 1
(Plays from Off-Off-Broadway)

Edited by
STANLEY NELSON
and
THE SMITH

NEW EGYPT / HORIZON

THE SCENE *is a joint project of* GNOSIS *and* THE SMITH, *two magazines, under the aegis of The Generalist Association, Inc. The cooperative imprint is New Egypt. This publication is intended as an annual record of dramatic creation. Its premise is that Off Off Broadway is the staging ground for the important innovations in drama, that the little theatres are equivalent to the little magazines as the launching points for new talent. This volume features a guide to Off Off Broadway as well as an introduction by Tom Tolnay, editor of* BACKSTAGE, *and all of the plays presented here were recently performed on Off Off Broadway.*

Stanley Nelson, Gnosis
Harry, The Smith
editors

The Gnosis participation in this project is assisted by a grant from New York State Council for The Arts, via Coordinating Council of Literary Magazines.

© Copyright October 15, 1972 by New Egypt. Volume I, complete. Published by The Generalist Association, Inc., 5 Beekman Street, New York, New York 10038.

Edited by Stanley Nelson and Harry Smith.

Printed at Liberal Press, 80 Fourth Ave., New York, New York.

$2.50 per copy. The Scene, 5 Beekman Street, New York, N. Y. 10038

Library of Congress Catalog Card Number 72-89382. Copyright © by The Scene. First printing, October, 1972.

Distributed by Horizon Press, 156 Fifth Ave., N.Y., N.Y. 10010

Contents

	Page
Introduction Tom Tolnay	5
Bang! Bang! David Newburge	10
Worms Roma Greth	33
Manitoba Guy Gauthier	65
Set It Down With Gold Frederick Bailey	79
Harrison Progressive School Stanley Nelson	86
Concentric Circles Benjamin Bradford	106
The Telegram Fran Lohman	140
The Heist Robert Reinhold	148
Dr. Franklin Eduardo Garcia	181
117 Off-Off Theatres	208

Photography Editors
FREDERICK BAILEY
MICHAEL CAMPIONE
STEVE GOLDBERG

Art Editor
AL INGEGNO

Cover Design
DICK HIGGINS

Off-Off-Broadway: An Introduction

BY TOM TOLNAY

Rarely in the history of theatre has the art been as abundant in one place and at one time as it is in the New York of the 1970s. And quantity, contrary to careless rumor, is often just as important as quality. For while great work has been known to spring up totally unattended—alone unto itself like a maple seedling that has managed to take root in the crack of a sidewalk—more often it's the product of a milieu of thought and expression. Whether a superior drama will emerge from the New York scene in this decade remains for the future to reveal, but certainly all the elements are there and some of them are in evidence in this book of plays.

The reference to theatrical wealth in New York is not the lavish costumes and elaborate sets and stylish talent of Broadway. Rather, it's the musty trunks of the city breeding theatre that threatens our codes, challenges the systems we live under, questions the dreams that guide us. That state of mind called off-off-Broadway—nicknamed OOB, the heir unapparent of off-Broadway.

In the 1960s, it was fashionable for writers connected with theatre to point to off-Broadway (a handful of houses at the time) as the fertile soil for development of theatre as art. Over the years, there were even productions to justify that kind of thinking. But Broadway's rising ticket prices—the result of blown up production costs and theatre rents, and greed for greater profit—created an economic

Tom Tolnay is editor of BACKSTAGE.

need for still another market-place: a lower priced, popular, stage
entertainment. Off-Broadway was chosen—and in a few years the
promoters sucked the ideas out of it, leaving it fallow.

Throughout much of that evolution, a flame of theatre burned dimly
but steadily in the cellars and lofts of the city. While Broadway was
entertaining thousands and off-Broadway was playing the role for
hundreds, other denizens of the theatre were performing for tens
virtually wherever they could find a few feet of flat space—so precious
in a town built straight up. Often young, usually idealistic, they
would recreate with astounding energy and dedication the works of
the great dramatists of the past, as well as those of current writers
with something to say (not to mention a sizeable number with noth-
ing whatsoever in their pens).

Oblivious to openings at Lincoln Center and closings on Broadway,
with little expectation of appreciation or financial gain, these artists
piece their productions together by hand and heart. Stage furniture
is saved from the garbage cans of the city. Props are collected from
their own rooms. Sets are built from scraps collected at construc-
tion and demolition sites. Costumes are sewn together from their
old clothing. A hand-made theatre from the first to the last act.

The substructure that is off-off-Broadway has not been constructed
by a single group; it's the kind of creature that must not be tagged
by the names of a few individuals or groups; it belongs to them all.
Many are part of the picture for only a few months. Others live
much of their adult lives off-off-Broadway. Many could easily be
tempted away with the prospect of funds and fame, but that doesn't
lessen what they have given. With ideas from some lives, the craft
of others, and the energy of them all, Off-off-Broadway has grown
up on its own creative fuel, motivated not by financial or personal
gain, but by a need for expression, a need for a personal theatre .

The vast variety of productions, quarters, and talent off-off-Broad-
way constitutes a remarkable force in art, one that is a dramatic

experience in itself. I have attended theatres in which there were no seats, broken ones, or cushions; have squatted on stairs to hear a Brooklyn accent whittle "Antigone" down to size; shivered in unheated lofts, sweated in stuffy basements for a few moving moments; half-dozed in a hollow-sounding school auditorium; heard hallowed church walls resound with "fuck you"; watched Ophelia drown herself in an East Village tenement; passed through the piss-stained curtains of a store-front theatre to hear backroom blasphemies; climbed three flights of stairs in yellow light to be spit at by a black actor who was either following directions or was just disgusted with the pigment of my face; have been offered pot, wine, knives; was coaxed onto more than one stage as a singing and/or dancing member of the troupe; have been invited to disrobe with the cast—and one night narrowly escaped being kidnapped!

OOB is life in the process of finding out what the hell it is all about. Many of the lives that make it up are so closely aligned to the idea of their stage that it's impossible to know where their everyday experience begins and their off-off-Broadway existence ends. Obviously not all of this experience—not all this "theatre"—is valuable. You take your chances. Amateurism is boldly thriving in some basements and lofts, and feeble theatrical wings have more than once carried some uncertain young or old writer or director over the audience so that he could shit on them. My head is stained with many such indignities. But there are at least an equal number of groups, units, gatherings, clubs, companies, repertories that are presenting substantial, exciting theatre on mean budgets and mighty talent.

My purpose is not to cut the wheat from the chaff. Nor could I. Off-off-Broadway is most exciting, most full of life, most nearly itself when left intact, whole, taken as raw goods right from the fields. Some make the mistake of taking in only one or two presentations downtown. Often they are put off—or put on—by the meanness of the productions and never return. What they have witnessed, however, is one or two small scenes in a play that is made up of many scenes and acts, one large condition of theatre. And it is the total experience that makes basement theatre stimulating and valuable.

Off-off-Broadway has managed to sustain itself—not feed its body, but its soul—while offering productions that are often free, or at a $1, $2, and $3 price scale. Sometimes the best a group has to offer is not worth a buck. Other times you will stagger away from the humble house permanently wounded by the experience. I have slinked out of off-off-Broadway theatres many times with my heart stuffed up my throat, or so angry at the playwright's reckoning that my fists were clenched. It was a good anger, the kind that teaches.

With a bit more attention being accorded off-off-Broadway theatre today, and with federal assistance to the arts increasing, OOB stands to better its financial condition somewhat. It can sure use it, the gods know. The deliverance of financial support, especially from the government, could have a nullifying effect on its art, could water down the motivation. But if OOB could survive the people, it certainly should be able to outlast a government of the people.

Off-off-Broadway no longer need be considered a proving ground for risky talent, though it continues to give new works and new directors an airing. But it also incorporates an art that can stand on its own, a theatre that is well developed, if not well equipped. Theatre must be judged by its talents rather than its accountrements. And genuine talent is plentiful off-off-Broadway, for it is a melting pot of visions from all over the country and the world. In fact some of its theatres and groups are better known in Europe than in their own city.

The plays from the nine writers in this collection—"The Heist" by Robert Reinhold; "Worms" by Roma Greth; "Bang Bang" by David Newburge; "Concentric Circles" by Benjamin Bradford; "Only A Play" by Eduardo Garcia; "The Telegram" by Fran Lohman; "Manitoba" by Guy Gauthier; "The Harrison Progressive School" by Stanley Nelson and "Set Down With Gold" by Frederick Baily— will attest to that abundance of talent better than any words I may put down here. You may not be taken in by all of the works in-cluded, but you must be excited by the variety of tone and expression they represent and the way these playwrights present their views of the world. The plays are a microcosm of the phenomenon that first gave them expression—off-off-Broadway. So read them here, then go see their work where it was born.

Bang! Bang!

BY DAVID NEWBURGE

BANG! BANG! was originally presented by Norman Hartman at the Old Reliable Theatre Tavern, 231 East 3rd Street, New York City, in July, 1969. The production was directed by Richard Lipton and featured the following actors:

COP	Irving Metzman
VERA	Valerie Paone
SNAY	Richard Lipton
HAKIM	Edward Barton

Approximate playing time: 40 minutes

Before a curtain, a POLICEMAN *stands stage center, waving his hands in traffic direction signals in a mock ballet to the tune of "Pizzicato" from "Sylvia." A* YOUNG GIRL, *wearing a cap over her short hair, and dressed in severe unflattering skirt and blouse enters stage right. She stands for a moment looking around. She eyes the* POLICEMAN *and after a moment decides to approach him. He doesn't notice her. She taps him on the arm.*

VERA: Excuse me. COP *doesn't notice her; continues directing traffic.* Excuse me.

COP: *continues directing traffic.* Yeah. What is it?

VERA: I'm the one you're looking for.

Al Ingegno

COP: I ain't looking for nobody.

VERA: But you are. And it's me.

COP: Look, lady. It's rush hour. Can't you see I'm busy here? Would you beat it? *He continues to direct traffic.*

VERA: *she reaches into her shopping bag and removes a pearl-handled revolver.* But I'm the one who shot those men. See?

COP: Jesus. *He looks at the gun in amazement, and drops his arms. Suddenly there is the sound of a terrible crash.* Christ! Now look what you did.

VERA: *meekly.* I'm sorry. I don't want to cause any trouble.

COP: *yells directions.* All right. Clear those wrecks out of here and make it snappy. You're tying up traffic. Move those bodies onto the sidewalk. *He motions his arms for the traffic to come around.* Help that woman off the jagged glass in Bonwit's window. Get that fag out of here giving mouth to mouth resucitation with his tongue. You, with the bracelet, beat it. Get those crying Girl Scouts out of the gutter—and sweep up those broken cookies. *Aside.* Yeh! two blocks down, two to the right, ask the manager for the key. *To the victims again.* Yeh! That's it, move that body. Yeh! All right now, everyone with blood on them raise their hands. *Stops, turns his attention back to* VERA. *Says through clenched teeth.* Gimme that gun! *She hands it over.* Okay. Now who did you shoot?

VERA: Randy Warble.

COP: That artist nut? The one with the silver hair?

VERA: *proudly.* It's on all the radio and TV stations. Even UHF.

COP: Any guy with silver hair probably has it coming. You really plugged him?

VERA: *nods energetically.* I'm Vera Milanos. Didn't you hear the news broadcasts?

COP: I've been on this beat all day. Out here I don't hear nothin' but horns and "Fuck you, Mack!" We did ask for radios but the Captain said—You're under arrest. You come with me. *He takes her arm and they start walking. They walk to stage right, then to stage left. Then to stage right again, back to center stage.*

VERA: Where are we going?

COP: You'll see when you get there. *She tries wrenching her arm from him.*

VERA: You're hurting my arm.

COP: Fabulous.

VERA: Brute. *Her voice rises in pitch.* Brute! *She screams.* FUCKING BRUTE!

As they get to center stage, the curtain opens. It is an austere room with three wooden benches, as in a court room or waiting room. One bench behind the other. He marches her in and sits her on the front bench.

COP: Wait here.

VERA: What for?

COP: Justice.

VERA: How long do I have to wait?

COP: Lady. I hope it takes you forever. *He walks to the back of the room, upstage and exists through a door closing it behind him.*

VERA *sits alone on the bench uncomfortably for a few moments. She looks around her fearfully and apprehensively. Finally, as she decides she is safe, she sits back on the bench and crosses her legs, ankle resting on knee in the masculine manner. Something swaggerish comes into her manner. She notices a large sign on the wall that says:* SMOKING PROHIBITED. *She reaches into her shopping bag and takes out a pack of cigarettes and matches. She looks at the sign boldly, defying it as she lights up. She shakes the match out and tosses it grandly on the floor in front of her.*

VERA: And I'm not sorry I did it either. You really had it coming. You son of a bitch. Three times I asked you for my script back. Three times you didn't pay any attention to me. You should have returned it baby. It was mine. You didn't have any right to keep it. Three times I said return it, and three times you didn't pay any attention to me. But you know that was a mistake now. Don't you Randy? I mean, people pay attention to Vera, or else. *Snaps her fingers.* Now you know. You really thought you could get away with anything. What could Vera do? Just a girl. Just a weak girl. But I proved who was strong. Didn't I baby? Hell, I'm more of a man than you are any day. *She laughs.* That look of surprise on your face when I pulled out the gun. *She mimics a high voice.* No, Vera. No. Don't do it. You were afraid, then. And the funny part is I wasn't even sure I would do it. Like it was half a joke, half serious. I didn't even know if I'd do it. Until you said. *High voice.* "No, Vera. No. Don't do it!" And then, baby — I just had to. I mean, there you were groveling in front of me like a worm. And I felt power. There was such power in my blood and bones that I just had to translate it into noise and pain. That crazy feeling. Up my chest, down my arm, down my finger, out the barrel. BANG! BANG! BANG! That loud satisfying blast of the gun. *She stops for a moment, closes her eyes and smiles blissfully.* I said satisfying, baby, and I meant it. Do you know, man, that when that cannon started roaring all my blood rushed through my system and gathered in one incredible tickling vortex of sensation, and I came. Yeah, baby. I came right in my jockies as I was letting you have it. Man, what a feeling. What joy! What pleasure! I never imagined that something groovy could happen between me and a man. But today, baby—For the first time— I felt it with you. *She pauses for a moment.* And you knew you were fucked good, too, didn't you, lying on the floor, your face white and twisted, moaning and thrashing about. Were you coming too? *Laughs.* I swear, for a second I almost felt sorry for you. Until that other guy started to come at me and I had to let him have it too. And then I heard others coming. So I ran, baby. I ran away, leaving behind my own little personal scene of carnage and destruction. Channel 2 says the bullets tore through your stomach and liver and spleen, and I think even a lung. Pretty good shooting for an amateur? Eh? Channel 4 says you're probably gonna die. Well, I hope so, Randy. If not. What was it all for? *She has run out of steam, and she curls up on the bench and pulls her cap over her eyes, trying to sleep. The door opens and the* COP *directs a thin, small* ARAB *into the room. He is dressed in slacks and an open shirt. He's about 25 years old.*

COP: Okay. Get in there you. Now you behave yourself while you're in here. *The* COP *removes the handcuffs from* HAKIM HAKIM *and closes the door.* HAKIM *doesn't see* VERA *and thinks himself alone.* HE *looks around.* VERA *sits up.*

VERA: Well, well. What have we got here. HAKIM *backs off in fright.* What are you in for? *He doesn't answer.* Cat got your tongue? *No answer.* Oh, fine. I can see this gonna be a cheery afternoon. They have to stick me with a creep. Okay. I'll try again. Hi, there. My name's Vera. What's yours, man?

HAKIM: Hakim. *He is backed into a corner.*

VERA: *she goes to him, hand outstretched, her attitude straightforward and masculine.* Pleased to meet you. *He shrinks back.* For Christ's sake. I'm not gonna eat you.

HAKIM: *In a polite, small voice—high pitched with a foreign accent.* Please. What time is it?

VERA: I don't have a watch. You got an appointment? What's the difference, anyhow. In here, one minute's the same as the next.

HAKIM: Please. I sit down. *He edges around her and moves toward the middle bench.*

VERA: Oh, sure, sure. Sit down. Make yourself at home. *He sits in the far corner of the middle bench watching her.* So tell me. What are you in for? *He stares at her. She approaches him menacingly and looks straight down at him.* I said, what are you in for?

HAKIM: I kill someone.

VERA: *feeling expansive and comradely.* No shit. Me too. What a terrific coincidence.

HAKIM: You kill someone too?

VERA: Well, any second now. Just as soon as he kicks off. But man. am I surprised. About you, I mean. I thought you might be in for snatching or something sneaky like that. I never dreamed you were a killer. You don't look the type.

HAKIM: The type?

VERA: No offense, meant. But a mousy little guy like you. I wouldn't have thought you'd have the guts. Who was it, your mother? The bitch? *He shakes his head.* The old man? The boss? *He shakes his head to each.* Come on, man. Don't keep me in suspense.

HAKIM: I kill deception. I kill treachery. A friend to the enemy who would destroy my people. But instead I destroy him. Through my hand, Allah has spoken. Through my hand, Allah has said death to the infidel.

VERA: Hallelujah! He speaks. Who was the old infidel?

HAKIM: His name was Kenneth. Robert Kenneth.

VERA: Not *the* Robert Kenneth.

HAKIM HAKIM: He who is no more. He who would rule the earth will now rule the grave. His subjects shall be the worms and maggots that eat his decaying flesh!

VERA: Bobby Kenneth. You killed Bobby Kenneth. I don't believe it. *She is stunned.*

HAKIM: Five shots through the head. Blood and brains pouring out thickly onto the carpet through smoking holes. *He puts his hands over his eyes as if to shut out the sight, and then shouts defiantly.* And I. I am the avenger.

VERA: No. I don't believe it. He was an all right guy. He was a great guy. As far as guys go. *She starts to cry.* How could you? You crummy little creep!

HAKIM: I am the savior of my people. I am the hope and the redemption.

VERA: *sobbing.* The one decent guy in the world. *The lights dim, and a spotlight picks up* HAKIM.

HAKIM: Two thousand people cheering in a hotel ballroom. Two thousand people calling "Hurray, Bobby. Bobby, we love you." Two thousand deluded fools, feeding the egotism of a power-mad despot. "I will help the poor," he said. But it was a lie. We are the poor, and it was not us who were his friends, but the rich Jews. How he courted the Jewish dollar and promised them the promised land. But there is no promised land. A land belongs to the people that has held it for centuries. To deliver a promised land to someone, you must take it from someone else. You must take it from its rightful owner, unless you are stopped. Unless someone dares to take a weapon in his hand and strike you down. But we will have it back, if we have to kill every Jew and Jew-lover on the face of the earth. *The lights come up.*

VERA: I just hope you get what's coming to you. *She gets up and goes over to him, making a fist.* I'd like to give it to you myself. *He flinches and crouches back.*

HAKIM: Are you a Jew?

VERA: What's wrong with Jews?

HAKIM: Thieves. Murderers.

VERA: Boy, I'd like to cut your balls off. *He shrinks back again. She laughs.* That really got to you, huh? You're afraid of that, huh? You're really afraid someone's gonna come along some day and cut off those balls. I bet they're not even much. Let's see 'em. *He doesn't move.* Come on, show 'em to me. I'll try not to laugh. *She reaches for his fly, but he shoves her hands away and runs across the room.*

HAKIM: *screams.* Filtmouth. Filth. Filth. Do not speak to me.

VERA: Don't worry, kid. I was just kidding around with you. I'm not really interested. I think men's sexual equipment is pretty God damn ugly, so I'm not too worked up about seeing yours.

HAKIM: Shut your filthmouth. I don't want to hear. I am pure. I am clean. You contaminate me with your filth.

VERA: You're pure! You're really pure at your age? You could never make it what a babe, huh?

HAKIM: You are a disgrace to the female sex. You profane the image of my mother.

VERA: Your mother? Christ. If every dame is like your mother to you, no wonder you're a virgin. *The door opens and the* COP *pushes a large, fortyish* MAN *through. The* MAN *is quarrelsome.*

SNAY: You just watch who you're shoving around, Mister. My lawyer's gonna hear about this. I'll have you up on so many charges you won't know what hit you.

COP: Sure, sure. I'm real worried.

SNAY: You cops think you can push people around. But I'm a citizen. I pay my taxes and I got my rights.

COP: Look. I don't want to have any more trouble out of you. *The* COP *removes* SNAY's *handcuffs and exits, locking the door behind him.*

SNAY: Fucking U.S. cops. One thing I'll say, those English cops are a damn sight more polite.

VERA: You sound like you've been around.

SNAY: Me? I've dealt with cops in half the countries of the Western World. And before I'm through I hope to cover the other half. Snay's my name. Herbert Martin Snay. Alias George Waldo Gibbs, alias Cuthbert Slotho Wilson, alias . . . Oh, shit, you can call me Herb.

VERA: *shakes hands with him.* I'm Vera Milanos.

SNAY: Vera Milanos. *The* Vera Milanos? *She smiles proudly.* The one who plugged the artist?

VERA: Uh huh.

SNAY: Hey. Pretty good. I heard the news come over the police car radio. You're a plucky little dame, eh?

VERA: *hardens.* I can do anything a man can do.

SNAY: Not anything, doll. Say, it's too bad you and me never met before. We coulda been a team. A regular Bonnie and Clyde. You coulda helped me rob banks and drugstores and—

VERA: Hey, wait a minute, I'm not a thief.

SNAY: It's easier than loading cargo. Hell I've been stealing since I found out the old lady's spare cash was hid under the sugar.

VERA: You have a warped criminal mind.

SNAY: *laughs appreciatively and nods his head.* Yeah. *He now notices* HAKIM—*and nods his head toward him.* And who's this guy? He don't say much, does he?

VERA: Once he gets started, it's hard to stop him.

SNAY: What's your name, kid? HAKIM *stares at him narrowly and doesn't answer.* SNAY *approaches him and clenches his fists.* I said what's your name, kid?

HAKIM: My name is Hakim.

SNAY: That's better. When I ask a question, I like an answer. Hakim, eh? What's that, your first name or your last name?

HAKIM: Both.

SNAY: Both?

HAKIM: My name is Hakim Hakim.

SNAY: That's a hell of a name. What are you an Arab or something?

HAKIM: I am from the Land of Jordan. I am, as you say, an Arab.

SNAY: Yeah. That's what I thought. The minute I laid eyes on you, I said to myself that guy's either an Arab or a nigger. I don't dig Arabs too much.

HAKIM: I am sorry.

SNAY: Nah. That's okay, kid. They're still better than niggers. The one thing I can't stand is niggers. I mean niggers is okay in their place—like if you need a shoeshine or a trunk carried. But these days you can't hardly find a nigger in his place. They all want to be in your place. Damn pushy bastards.

VERA: Snay. Snay. Now I know. You're the guy who shot that Civil Rights Leader.

SNAY: *belligerently.* Well you just let 'em try and prove it.

VERA: Come on, now. We're all killers and you gotta tell us.

SNAY: You mean that little jerk-off is a killer. Come on, no.

VERA: He is, man. The little crumb killed Bobby Kenneth.

SNAY: *whistles.* No kidding. Well, I'll be damned. You know, I was thinking of doing that myself. That guy liked niggers.

VERA: You did it, didn't you. You shot that Negro.

SNAY: Talk to my lawyers.

VERA: Who am I gonna tell?

SNAY: Okay. I'm not admitting anything, see—but if that guy got it—so what? He needed to be taught a lesson. I mean that last Freedom March. Hell, that was just one Freedom March too many. He was trying people's patience. Marching all those niggers through white neighborhoods, tying up decent law-abiding traffic. I mean someone was gonna give it to him sooner or later. So the cops pick on me. Just because I've been in and out of reform schools and prisons since I'm ten. But I led 'em a merry chase all right. From state to state, from country to country. It took 'em a while to catch me.

HAKIM: Christian Dog. You are no better than the Jews. With all your talk of love and charity, it is you who are the oppressors of the world. It is you who ride the backs of the sick, the poor, and the black to proclaim your white supremacy. The blacks who at last are turning from the false Christian Gods to Allah, the true and only God. And you murder us. *He rushes at* SNAY, *fists flying crazily.* SNAY *pushes him onto a bench with one hand.*

SNAY: What's he crazy?

VERA: He's a religious fanatic. HAKIM *sobs hysterically.*

SNAY: He's a nut. At least you and me see things more alike. Eh, baby? *He nudges her.*

VERA: We don't see anything alike.

SNAY: Sure we do, baby. We're both white ain't we? Hey, you know, I bet we could see a lot more than that, too. Just give it a try. *He grabs her. She pulls away.*

VERA: Don't touch me.

SNAY: Come on, baby. We'll have a little fun. I got hot nuts.

VERA: *she screams.* Don't touch me. I can't stand to be touched by men.

SNAY: Oh, I get it. You're a dyke ain't ya? I'll use my tongue if you want, baby. But you don't know what you're missing.

VERA: Any man that gets in me is gonna pay for it.

SNAY: Oh shit, a hooker. But that's okay. I'm not proud. I've paid before. With me it doesn't have to be for love. A fuck is a fuck.

VERA: You men should all die. Every one of you. Die. Pigs. Put yourself upon women and use us for foul disgusting things. To you we're just something to help you get your dirty rock off.

SNAY: It's better than my fist, baby. How's about let's give it a try. You might even like it. I bet you got a sweet little box there. One that ain't been used and stretched too much. *He goes after her.*

VERA: *backs away.* Get away from me.

SNAY: Aw, come on now. Be nice. Just a quick one. We'll let the Arab kid watch.

VERA: Pig! Pig! Pig! *She reaches into her shopping bag, pulls out another gun and blasts him three times point blank. He stops for a moment, then laughs.*

SNAY: You don't think you can get rid of me that easy now, do you? I mean . . . ugh . . . in this world somebody's got to decide who lives or dies. And I decide baby. I'm a hunter, not a pigeon. I'm immune to that kind of thing. I've had my shots.

VERA: *with vicious hate, through clenched teeth.* Just don't touch me.

SNAY: Sure baby. I'll leave you alone. I can take a hint. Who needs you? I been in prison plenty and I know how to get my rocks off without a dame. *Looks at* HAKIM. Come here, kid. HAKIM *looks terrified*. Come here, kid. Don't be afraid. Let's you and me be friends.

HAKIM: I don't want to be your friend. SNAY *puts his arm around* HAKIM.

SNAY: Sure you do, kid. Say we both get convicted and sentenced up the river. Why a skinny little guy like you wouldn't have a chance in one of those prisons. Those cons'd have your ass up in the air so fast, you won't know what hit you. Now, you'll need a friend to protect you and take care of you and look after you. HAKIM *pulls away*. I'm willing to do that for you, so what's the big deal. *Takes a candy bar from his pocket*. Here, kid. Have a Hershey bar. HAKIM *shakes his head*. Come on. It's for you. We'll be pals.

HAKIM: No!

SNAY: Why, you little fairy crumb. Playing hard to get, eh? Who're you kidding? Everybody knows all you Arabs like to take it up the ass. You don't even know what you're turning down. I've got a big one, baby. Come here. Feel it. *He grabs* HAKIM's *hand and puts it on his crotch*. HAKIM *pulls his hand away and reaches into his pocket. He pulls out a revolver and blasts* SNAY *several times*. Well, it looks like we've got a lot of big shooters around the table. Fuck you both. I'm gonna do some shooting of my own. I'll do it myself. *He goes off to a corner, faces the wall and masturbates.*

VERA: *Reaches into her shopping bag for a sheaf of papers and steps forward, addressing the empty court as her audience.* All right girls. All right girls. Let's settle down now. First I'd like to take this opportunity to thank all you groovy chicks for attending. I want to introduce you to an organization that will change your lives. My organization, MAIM, The Militant Association for Intimidating Men. MAIM! Today let me give you a small idea of our program's motives and aims. Later you can read about it in detail in this 200-page pamphlet which I shall pass out free to all girls at the end of the meeting. Should one of the enemy wish a copy, the price will be five dollars, which will go into our castration fund. To begin with, since the dawn of man, woman has been repressed by the so-called stronger sex. But girls, the time has come for the Dawn of Woman. By pure physical force we have been enslaved and subjected to every kind of torture and humiliation at the hands of the great Phallus. Right? Right? And why? Because of a slight muscular inferiority, our superior minds and souls have been shut away and chained, while men have run amuck bringing hate, war, and destruction to the world. But girls, we must fight fire with fire. If we are to save the world, we must temporarily overcome our natural sensitivity and reticence. We must use the enemy's tools against them. *We* must kill, *we* must maim, *we* must destroy. We must declare ourselves separate and superior and challenge the Masculine Sex to out and out war. Until the only men to survive are in chains, slaves to the glorious will of womankind, their only purpose to furnish the seed necessary to propagate the future of our victory. Only then will the world again be the Garden of love and beauty it can and must be. Let those worms not enslave us with the myth of romantic love. There is no love between man and woman. There is only hate, war, and destruction. Arise Amazons. Cast off your fetters. Then, and only then, will we have the ultimate triumph. I will now pass out my pamphlet which I hope all you girls will study carefully. Girls. MAIM needs more members. Up to now, I'm the ony one. I can't save the world alone. We've got to expand and open chapters all over the country, all over the world. MAIM needs disciples with fearless hearts and unwavering loyalty. Yeah, MAIM needs zealots, killers, martyrs, castraters. Step forward girls, easy now, in a line, form a line, please. OK who's first? Give me your name, address and telephone number.

SNAY: Knock it off will you, butch. How can I concentrate. *Back still to audience, trying to masturbate. Says to himself*: Big round tits. Nice pink nipples. Round ass. Nice tight pussy.

VERA: Here you are girls—Exhibit A. He isn't even good for the things he's good for.

SNAY: Oh, shit. *He zips up and turns forward.* I'll do it later.

VERA: You can't make it, baby. You can't make it. I knew it all along. You're a Eunuch. All talk and no erection. You're not even a man. *Laughs viciously.*

SNAY: Don't say that.

VERA: My clit's probably bigger and stiffer than your cock.

SNAY: *Starts to shadow box.* Okay put 'em up. You're gonna get a shot in the mouth.

VERA: Mr. Softcock. Mr. Softcock. Got to prove he's a man with his fists, cause his cock won't get hard.

SNAY: *He goes crazy.* I'll fix you. *He takes a gun out of his pocket and shoots her. Nothing happens.*

VERA: Shit, man. It's like you said. You can't kill a killer.

SNAY: I said that didn't I. You can't kill a killer. SNAY *and* VERA *begin to revel in their new found immortality.* THEY *shoot each other with their fingers like kids, playing cops and robbers, become hysterical with laughter, fall into each other's arms, slap each other on the back and dance around.* THEY *generally act like two long-lost lodge brothers at a convention.*

VERA: Hate lives, man. Only the good's interred with the bones.

HAKIM: *Starts to cry.* Why am I here. I don't want to be here. Not with you. I don't want to be here with you. Mama. Mama.

SNAY: That snotty kid don't like our company. Maybe we're a little too rough for him, eh?

VERA: Whatsa matter, sissy boy? HAKIM *raises his gun and shoots her.*

SNAY: Killers have got to have guts, kid. Killers don't fold up and cry for their mamas. You're giving us a bad name.

HAKIM: I want to go home. I want to go home. *The lights narrow, and a spotlight falls on* HAKIM. Home. A mud hut in a very distant land. The walls flaking with dust and age. Behold. A woman lies on her back sweating in pain, her damp upper lip pulled back to expose brown and rotting teeth. This woman is about to bring forth into the world her fifth and favorite child. A man-child fragile and intense. A man-child destined . . .

VERA: *Spotlight picks her up on another part of the stage.* You're gonna have a new daddy, Vera, she told me. What the fuck did I want a new dady for. Didn't my own daddy do enough harm? Coming home soused silly every Goddamn night, slamming me black and blue, hating my guts just cause I *was*. Me, the little knock-up that forced the poor slob to marry that stupid bitch my mother.

SNAY: My old lady scrubbed floors in office buildings, just like some Nigger woman. We lived in the slums of St. Louis, but they wasn't so bad till the Niggers moved in and took 'em over. Then those buildings really went to hell. I mean they live like pigs, like Goddamn barnyard pigs. If there's one thing I can't stand it's filth. My mother's place was scrubbed so clean you could eat off the floor. She used to come home at 3 a.m. from scrubbing those office buildings, and get right back down on her knees to scrub the flat. I used to watch her. We woulda moved like everybody else when the niggers come, but we just didn't have the dough. I swore right there and then that one day I was gonna have dough. Plenty of it. And I wasn't gonna work like no nigger for it. Sure I rob banks. Why the fuck not? It ain't hurtin' nobody but some lousy big insurance company. And anyway, you gotta have brains to be a bank robber. You don't see no nigger bank robbers. You don't just walk in and say stick 'em up like in the movies. You gotta sit down, and plan. You gotta draw up maps and figure everything out perfect, so you don't get caught. Course I did get caught a few times.

HAKIM: As the years passed, it became clear to me that I was special. That I had been born with a divine purpose, to carry through Allah's will on Earth. But not only was I myself aware of this difference. It was evident also to the ignorant peasantry of my village, who shunned and rejected what they did not understand and thus feared. And so it was that this child of Allah knew loneliness. A loneliness so deep and complete as to eclipse any loneliness ever felt before by man. On all the Earth, there was no one to turn to but my adoring and blessed mother. Yet through this complete isolation I came to understand pain and suffering. Not only my own, but of all my people. And these cruel ignorants who had hurt me so deeply would one day venerate me as the Child of Allah, the redeemer. I knew the day would come when I would triumph over injustice and save the poor and the downtrodden. I knew the day would come when, when . . .

VERA: So she married him. My new daddy. She married him because she was a bitch in heat and had to stuff her hot cunt. And he could fill it. Man, he was a big bozo. *That's* what she really liked about him. God knows it wasn't his personality. And he was always taking every chance he could get to show it off in front of me. I mean, he was sick, man. Here I was a skinny ten-year old, and this creep, my new daddy, digs nothing so much as showing off his cock to me. Like he'd go into the bathroom and leave the door sort of accidentally half-open. And he'd sit there for an hour or so, playing with himself. Every once in a while he'd look up to make sure I was watching. Sure I was watching. I was fascinated. But not cause I wanted his, like he thought. Cause I wanted one for myself. I should have had one. I was cheated! And then he'd like walk around with his fly open all day. The zipper broke, hah hah. Or after dinner he'd sit there and watch television in his boxer shorts and it would be dripping through the opening. And the stupid bitch my mother never caught on what it was all about. *Mimics high voice.* Put yourself back in, she'd say, giggling. It's not nice in front of the child. And he'd sort of half tuck it back in, fondling first, his eyes gazing into mine.

SNAY: I mean Niggers are meant to do menial work. Not whites. Those fucking prison guards made me work in the laundry. Me, working in the laundry with a bunch of dirty niggers.

HAKIM: And the Jews moved in like locusts devouring the land, forcing thousands of my people to leave their homes. To leave the land that had been their's for centuries. The Jews! Crushing my poor and simple people with money and technology. One day I will lead my people in revolt, and we will drive out these foreign invaders. Would that they all had died in Hitler's incinerators.

VERA: So one day the stupid bitch goes out for the evening and leaves him to babysit. Babysit! Get that? He comes up to my room where I'm sleeping, and shakes me. I open one eye, and the first thing I see is IT, hanging out of the boxers balls and all. He sees I'm awake and the whole thing gets hard. Christ it was like a baton. Touch it, he says. No, I says, but he puts my hand on it and holds it there. Okay, now suck it, he says. Put your mouth on it and suck it. I kept my teeth closed and shook my head. Suddenly he wallops me on the jaw. My mouth flies open and he shoves it in. I'm choking and gagging, but he holds my head down on it. So I sucked until that horrible stuff shot out into my mouth. SHE *gets hysterical.* And I had to swallow it. He made me swallow it.

SNAY: Why that bastard. Ain't that just like a nigger.

HAKIM: And the American Politicians must be destroyed. The American Politicians who hear only the voice of Jewish Money and not the agonized cries of poverty.

SNAY: So I went into this bank to case the joint. And this big nigger guard standin' there keeps looking at me. You could see he thought he was better than me. Fucking nigger, better than me. There ain't no nigger better than me. I'm white, man. I'm king.

VERA: An hour later he got it up again and fucked me. That big thing tearing into my insides, making me bleed. A ten year old kid. *Starts to cry.* I hate 'em. I'd like to kill every one of em'. They should all die.

SNAY: You know in ten years this country ain't gonna be fit to live in. They're taking over everything. I mean they're everywhere. Turning the best neighborhoods into slums, taking good decent jobs away from white men. I'd like to ship every last one of them black bastards back to Africa where they come from, elsewise this country ain't gonna be fit for shit.

HAKIM: Help the poor, he said. Don't you understand, he was greedy for power. He would have been President of America, and destroyed you, my people. I am the Savior. I am the second coming of Mohammed. *To his followers:* Wait—come back.

VERA: You took my script, Randy. My blood and guts on paper. You told me you were gonna make a movie of it. But a year went by, almost two, and nothing ever seemed to happen. I asked you to give it back to me and you wouldn't. It was my only copy, Randy, and I wanted it back, I begged you and you wouldn't listen. You just kept putting me off. I said give it back or I'll kill you, and you laughed at me. Well you're not laughing at me now Randy. You didn't think I'd really do it. And you're just the first.

SNAY: I stood up on this roof, see. I had this high-powered rifle. I aimed it real careful, lined him up right between the eyes. Die you uppity nigger. I'm gonna put you down for good. This here's white country and it's gonna stay white. Let you have your way, and in three generations the whole country'll be nigger. A lot of people say they don't feel nothin' when they kill someone. But I did man. When that bullet blew the back of his head off . . . bliss man, bliss. I blow your ass off motherfucker. I blow your ass off motherfucker. I'll cut you. I'll cut you. Ha! I blew you so hard, I made you white! You hear motherfucker, I made you white. Pow! Ping. Splat. Hell, man. No hard feelings. I didn't even know you. I only did it for my country.

VERA: Women are kind. Women are gentle. The spirit of Motherhood moves them in ways of love. Men are creatures of death, and by death they must be consumed. I swear I'll save and protect the future of womanhood from the tyrannical and despotic cock. So help me God, I swear it. I swear it.

SNAY: Hey, Arab. You know you sort of look a little like a nigger. You got nigger blood? HAKIM *raises his tommy gun and shoots* SNAY. SNAY *fires back.*

VERA: Fucking pig men. Insensitive brutes. SHE *shoots both* HAKIM *and* SNAY. THEY *shoot her back.*

HAKIM: Jewlovers! Oppressors! I kill for God.

VERA: I kill for mother.

SNAY: I kill for country.

VERA: Cocksuckers. *Shoots man in the face.*

SNAY: *Follows her example—finds a Negro.* For you, Niggers. *Shoots man in the face.*

HAKIM: Filthy Jew bastards. *Shoots him in face.*

VERA, SNAY, HAKIM: *Together, in unison.* Black Sambo. Mother-raper. Jewcunt. Coon boy. Yidfuck. *Stop, drop their guns, continue much more softly.* Up your ass. Up your twat. Suck. Fartface. Shit ass. Rat fuck. Vomithead. Pissmouth.

CURTAIN

Worms

BY ROMA GRETH

WORMS was originally present-
ed by Viktor Allen at the Omni
Theater Club, Inc., 145 West
18th Street, New York City, in
November, 1970. The production
was directed by Viktor Allen and
featured the following actors:

DOROTHY . . . . Lisa Mayo
MADONNA . . . . Connie Clark

Approximate playing time: 30 minutes

The room is undefined . . . shifting . . . there are many shadows de-
spite three or four unshaded light bulbs hanging from bare black wires
across the center of the stage. There is toward the rear of this room
the illusion of great depth or length, almost like a cave or a hole with
bare light bulbs growing smaller in the distance. Filling this area are
outlines of large bins. One of these is real and solid and directly Up
Center. It stands on wooden legs and is painted white, but has a
home-made, unfinished look about it as if it has been hammered to-
gether from odds and ends. The bin is full of soil which cannot,
however, be seen because of the fairly high boards forming the sides
of the bin. Around the edges of the room are smaller bins, resembling
the large one. Somewhere is a table, perhaps just a card table, on which

stand some round containers similar to those used to package pints of ice cream. There are holes punched in the lids of these. There is an old radio on the counter-table, rather the worse for wear. There is also a sign which says: BOXES OF 25: $1 — 100 LOTS: $2.50. *Two old chairs are behind the table. There are two home-made signs hanging in the room. One says:* QUIET! WORMS SLEEPING *and the other:* NESTOR'S WORM RANCH. *There is a door at one side of the stage, a fairly massive door which firmly seals off a world of sunshine — for the colors of this room are black and grey and dim mauve. . . . Humming, Dorothy Nestor enters carrying a large, battered pot containing mashed potatoes. Dorothy is a large woman of indeterminate age. Her hair is cropped short, her face plain. She wears dungarees, a tailored old blouse over which is a man's shirt of heavy material, worn like a coat or sweater and open in the front.*

DOROTHY: Dinnertime! Come and get it! *Banging on the pot with a big old spoon.* Soup's on! *She splats a wad of potato-mix into one of the smaller bins.* Okay, guys, eat hearty! Mashed potatoes for everybody! *Looking into the bin with a grin.* Ah ha! Like that, don't you? Ummmmm. Look at them go. Here, have some more. *She splats in another wad.* Ahhhhh . . . down the old hatch, boys. Don't be afraid to take seconds. It'll make you grow great, big, and fat. *Going to another bin and splatting potatoes into that.* Plenty for all. Hey — Hey, J. Edgar, let those little worms alone! They have to grow big and fat too, you know. We don't want any skinny guys around here. *Going to the large bin.* Well, did you fellows think I was going to forget you? No, sir. Here you are! *Dumping the rest of the pot into the bin.* Go to it, gang. Eat it all up. Congressmen, don't be bashful. *Looking into bin.* I'll be damned. *Reaching in and picking up a large worm.* What's the matter with you, Ted? Lost something? Like your appetite? Or aren't mashed potatoes good enough? Okay, okay. Tomorrow we'll have a special treat — oatmeal! *Putting the worm into the bin again.* Now get back in the compound with the rest of the family and don't complain. It's not as though you're paying guests. *Thoughtfully.* Of course, in a way you are paying. When you get

just a little bigger somebody is going to stick a sharp hook right
through you. Right through that soft, slippery, cool worm skin of
yours and into those grey-white insides and you're going to squirm
around on that hook while you're dipped into water. You'll be smoth-
ering and wriggling and the hook will be cutting your little insides.
Then — snap! Into a fish's mouth? Now go on — eat. McLuhan,
quit bothering those young worms! . . . You'd better all be good or
I'll let the red mites get you. And then you'll have to be flushed and
you won't like that. *Straightening with a tired sigh.* Ah . . . I think
that's the last of it — Let's see . . . worked from back to front to-
night . . . forty-five bins . . . yes. Ought to be just in time for the
news. *She glances at her watch as she sets down the pot.* Oh, my god!
She slaps the watch, listen to it tick. Damn! I'm missing my news!
*Dorothy immediately becomes animated, dashes to the old radio,
turns it on, spins the dial, bangs the radio impatiently when it does
not start right away. A news commentator is finally heard.*

VOICE: — garden clubs of the Tri-County area will hold their con-
vention here in June. Their theme will be: BEAUTY AND LOVE IN THE
WORLD OF SUNSHINE ABOVE.

DOROTHY: *Disgusted* Crap.

VOICE: One of the highlights of the conference will be a tour of
Point Park to observe the displays of hybrid roses.

DOROTHY: Roses! Damn! Don't tell me I missed all the good stuff
tonight. *Dorothy impatiently spins the radio dial and this time finds
a voice reciting actual news which can be taped from any paper.
This news should be the latest happenings, with as much emphasis
on violence as possible.*

DOROTHY: *With satisfaction.* Ahhhhhhh. . . .

The newscast continues with stories of war, crime, or death until it is well established that this a recital of horrors which Dorothy Nestor is obviously enjoying. She listens avidly, hanging over the radio so that she does not miss a single detail, oblivious to everything else. Madonna Miller enters and stands uncertainly, taking in the scene with a kind of horror of her own. Madonna is a fairly young woman, fragile and pale, with large eyes and dark hair. Her dress is modern, but not outstanding, chosen perhaps with the hope of conformity.

MADONNA: *After a moment.* Excuse me. *Louder since Dorothy is so involved with her radio.* Excuse me! EXCUSE ME!

DOROTHY: *Turning.* Oh.

MADONNA: I came to —

DOROTHY: We're closed.

MADONNA: But it said on the door that —

DOROTHY: Did I forget to turn the damn sign again? *She strides right by Madonna, yanks open the door and reverses a sign which says "Open" to the "Closed" side, then closes the door with a finality which sends Madonna farther into the room.* Now then. We're closed.

MADONNA: But I must —

DOROTHY: And I'm listening to my favorite program.

MADONNA: The news?

DOROTHY: You know it. Shh!

Dorothy runs back to the radio and turns it up loud so that a particularly grotesque item can be plainly heard.

VOICE: *After the completion of this item.* And that concludes our six o'clock newscast. Tune in again tomorrow for —

DOROTHY: Damn! I missed almost all of it.

VOICE: — the latest happenings at home and abroad. *A woman's voice is heard.* Ladies, do you have trouble getting grass stains out of your daughter's blouses — ?

DOROTHY: *Snapping off the radio.* I got carried away tonight. Talking to the worms. When I do that I never get finished feeding in time to hear the whole broadcast.

MADONNA: But it's so —

DOROTHY: What?

MADONNA: Horrible.

DOROTHY: It's news.

MADONNA: Bad news.

DOROTHY: Semantics.

MADONNA: What?

DOROTHY: Semantics. Good. Bad. Depends who you're talking to.

MADONNA: But there's so much —

DOROTHY: Like we kill the Communists, that's good. The Communists kill us, that's bad.

MADONNA: — death.

DOROTHY: What?

MADONNA: I said there's always so much death in the news. And dying.

DOROTHY: Just as much living.

MADONNA: No.

DOROTHY: The living are the ones killing the dying, aren't they? So it's not just Death. Look. Forty-five soldiers get shot in the gut. Okay, so much for them. They're dead. But how about the guy on the other end of the gun? He's had a successful day. He can put his marks on the wall, pat himself on the back and have a good supper. Maybe even get a medal. Don't tell me that's not living!

MADDONNA: That's horrible.

DOROTHY: That's survival.

MADONNA: I never listen to that sort of thing.

DOROTHY: Then you also miss all the news about the flower conventions. Did you know they're having one in the Tri-County area in June?

MADONNA: Really? I love flowers.

DOROTHY: Well, honey, you came to the wrong place. This ain't no flower shop.

MADONNA: I know.

DOROTHY: And, besides, we're closed.

MADONNA: No! Please —

DOROTHY: Come back tomorrow. I open at nine.

MADONNA: I must have some worms tonight!

DOROTHY: And I have to get my supper.

MADONNA: Surely it wouldn't take more than a minute to sell me —

DOROTHY: Business is business, lady.

MADONNA: But —

DOROTHY: I'm closed.

MADONNA: I mean, I know how men are, but —

DOROTHY: Men? I thought we were talking about worms.

MADONNA: You said you had to get supper and I said I know how men are —

DOROTHY: I only have to get supper for myself.

MADONNA: You're not married?

DOROTHY: Was.

MADONNA: Oh.

DOROTHY: Barney's been feeding the worms for six years now.

MADONNA: I don't understand . . .

DOROTHY: Himself.

MADONNA: You mean he's — Oh, dear.

DOROTHY: The wild worms, that is. I bet they enjoyed Barney.

MADONNA: Er — Sure if you have no one to cook for anymore, you could take just another minute to —

DOROTHY: You're married.

MADONNA: Oh — yes.

DOROTHY: And it's important to rush home for supper if you're married but if you're not it's okay to go hungry.

MADONNA: I didn't mean that.

DOROTHY: Some people remind me of worms.

MADONNA: All right! Just sell me a few and I'll get out of here.

DOROTHY: My . . .

MADONNA: What?

DOROTHY: You're real uptight, aren't you?

MADONNA: I . . . Yes, I guess I am.

DOROTHY: Well, now. That's just too bad. Tell you what I'll do! I'll give you a sample worm to tide you over until you can pick up your order tomorrow. *Dorothy abruptly roots a worm from the bin and throws it at Madonna who leaps backward with a scream, bumps into another bin, dashes away, nearly runs into another and ends up far from the door, huddling within herself, frantically trying to stay as far from the bins as possible. Dorothy laughs.*

DOROTHY: I thought you wanted a worm.

MADONNA: No! Yes . . . I . . . Please! Don't do it again!

DOROTHY: I knew you were one.

MADONNA: One — what?

DOROTHY: One of those people who's afraid of worms. I can tell you guys every time. You come in and want to hang right around the door. You have a fit if you even have to get near one of the bins.

MADONNA: Well — they might come out.

DOROTHY: People are so dumb about worms. Look, now these bins are full. And they keep getting more full all the time. Like thousands of worms. All sizes. But as long as those lights are lit, the worms won't ever come out. They'll stay right where they are. But the lights have to be on day and night.

MADONNA: Really . . .?

DOROTHY: Worms can't see, but their skin is very sensitive to light. They were made for dark places. Holes, caves, the underside. Everything has an underside, you know.

MADONNA: *Looking around.* This is . . . inverted.

DOROTHY: I like that. The inverted . . . the underside. The place of worms. Yes . . . Anyway, you turn out those lights and you know what happens?

MADONNA: No.

DOROTHY: Thousands of worms will ooze over the sides of these bins, down onto the floor. Like water over a dam . . . a flood of worms. You see, the bins are just this big — they can't grow but as long as I keep feeding them the worms keep breeding. Handfuls of worms just waiting for darkness so they can get out and hunt room to breathe. If I'd turn out those lights you'd soon be knee deep in worms. And they're slippery. They'd pile up around your legs like water rising. Tides of worms. You'd slip — fall down into them. Through them — worms oozing over your face, into your mouth, your ears.

MADONNA: Stop it!

DOROTHY: It happened once. The lights were turned out by mistake. One time when Barney was sick. Of course, nobody was in here then. They finally came oozing out the door, the undulation of thousands of worms forcing it open, gushing down the lane . . . We had worms as far away as the highway. Some of my customers came over and scooped them up by the bucketful.

MADONNA: I don't want to hear about it!

DOROTHY: Um — ?

MADONNA: Open the door.

DOROTHY: Can't.

MADONNA: Let some daylight into this place!

DOROTHY: Day light is dry. The worms need to be damp.

MADONNA: Don't tell me any more about worms!

DOROTHY: . . . You know, I'm glad I'm not as flakey as some of my customers.

MADONNA: I'm — sorry. I guess it's hard for somebody to understand who's . . . in the business. It's just — I don't think there's anything in this world I'm more scared of than — worms.

DOROTHY: Then what are you doing here?

MADONNA: They — my son wants some.

DOROTHY: He and his Daddy are going fishing tonight.

MADONNA: No. It's his birthday. Stevie's birthday.

DOROTHY: Huh?

MADONNA: Well, he wants — worms for his birthday.

DOROTHY: No kidding?

MADONNA: He has this — he likes — bugs and things. He always has. He likes to watch them and — even keep them for pets. He has — quite a collection.

DOROTHY: Where?

MADONNA: We have a room in the garage. I never go out there.

DOROTHY: Come here.

MADONNA: No.

DOROTHY: Oh, come on. If you got a kid with a bug complex, you might as well get used to them.

MADONNA: I never could.

DOROTHY: That's what you think. Until I met my husband I was just like you. But married to a guy like Barney you get used to them. What a sense of humor he had! I was always finding worms in the darndest places — my shoes, pots and pans, my douche bag —

MADONNA: Didn't you just die?

DOROTHY: No. I didn't. Look.

MADONNA: Don't — throw another one at me!

DOROTHY: I promise.

MADONNA: Thank you.

DOROTHY: If you come here and look.

MADONNA: But I —

DOROTHY: Otherwise . . . *Reaching into the bin.*

MADONNA: I'll scream!

DOROTHY: Go ahead. But I don't know what good it's going to do you. I live alone out here. All the fishermen who come have gone on over to the lake or home or someplace.

MADONNA: Oh. . . .

DOROTHY: Just come here and look, will you?

MADONNA: *Slowly and fearfully approaching a bin, not too close, hardly daring to look, finally peeping, then looking in.* I don't see anything.

DOROTHY: That's why I told you to look. So what's all the fuss about? Nothing but soil in there.

MADONNA: What's the white stuff that looks like mashed potatoes?

DOROTHY: Mashed potatoes.

MADONNA: What's it doing in there?

DOROTHY: What do you do with mashed potatoes?

MADONNA: . . . Eat them.

DOROTHY: Well?

MADONNA: Oh.

DOROTHY: Now doesn't that make worms seem more human?

MADONNA: Not really.

DOROTHY: I guess you're a hopeless case.

MADONNA: That's what John says.

DOROTHY: Your husband.

MADONNA: Yes.

DOROTHY: Why does he think you're a hopeless case?

MADONNA: I'm keeping you from your supper —

DOROTHY: I thought we'd decided that since I'm a widow I can eat any time.

MADONNA: We didn't decide anything.

DOROTHY: Maybe we will. Later.

MADONNA: What?

DOROTHY: Doesn't John want his supper?

MADONNA: We ate early.

DOROTHY: Oh?

MADONNA: As soon as he came from work. He likes that.

DOROTHY: After which he sent you out here to buy worms.

MADONNA: Not exactly.

DOROTHY: Don't tell me it was your idea.

MADONNA: No . . . Well — Stevie — insisted. I gave him a a game and he had a party this afternoon but . . . he was crying and John wouldn't come out to get worms —

DOROTHY: Maybe John doesn't think worms are much of a birthday present.

MADONNA: No, it's just. . . .

DORMOTHY: What?

MADONNA: Oh, what does it matter? I'm tired. I'm so tired from that awful party with children hollering and balloons popping and — Just sell me some worms, will you?

DOROTHY: Umm — I don't think so.

MADDONA: I don't know how you stay in business.

DOROTHY: I'm near a state park and a lake.

MADONNA: You'd never get away with your attitude if you weren't!

DOROTHY: Listen, lady, it's after hours. I'm tired too, you know. Raising worms is hard work and I have to do it all since Barney's gone. I have to relax sometimes too, you know.

MADONNA: I guess I wasn't really thinking —

DOROTHY: Now wait. You want to relax with me awhile, maybe I'll give you some worms.

MADONNA: *Starting to go.* I don't want to hang around this terrible place!

DOROTHY: Then go.

MADONNA: There must be another place around this lake that sells worms.

DOROTHY: They're all closed now.

MADONNA: Oh.

DOROTHY: *Watching her as she turns back from the door without touching it.* My. I didn't know worms could ever be that important to anybody.

MADONNA: He — Stevie screams if he doesn't have his way.

DOROTHY: Doesn't his Daddy ever spank him?

MADONNA: He doesn't scream for his Daddy.

DOROTHY: I'm Dorothy Nestor.

MADONNA: Oh. Mrs. Miller. Madonna Miller.

DOROTHY: *Getting a bottle from beneath the table.* Have some wine, Madonna.

MADONNA: No, thank you.

DOROTHY: Oh, come on. If I'm not going to eat right away, a little wine will give me a pick-up.

MADONNA: But I —

DOROTHY: And I never did like to drink alone.

MADONNA: But —

DOROTHY: It's not worm wine if that's what you're thinking.

MADONNA: Oh, I never thought they made —

DOROTHY: *Pressing a glass on her.* They don't.

MADONNA: Well — thank you.

DOROTHY: *Watching her take a swallow.* Of course it has one small worm in the bottom to give it flavor.

MADONNA: *Dropping her glass.* God!

DOROTHY: You didn't have to do that. It's very expensive stuff. Imported from Mexico. Like Mexican jumping beans. That's a worm too, you know.

MADONNA: Yes, I — know.

DOROTHY: Have some more.

MADONNA: No — thank you — I —

DOROTHY: You have a crazy name.

MADONNA: Well — Mother thought it would be a nice good name.

And she said I could always shorten it to just plain "Donna" if I didn't like it.

DOROTHY: But you do.

MADONNA: Well, it is different. *Laughing a little.* It's nice to have — something distinctive, isn't it?

DOROTHY: Even if it's only a name.

MADONNA: Now really —

DOROTHY: I'm not like you, Madonna.

MADONNA: No, you don't seem —

DOROTHY: I buried the man I married.

MADONNA: I don't want to bury John.

DOROTHY: Want him to bury you?

MADONNA: No!

DOROTHY: In marriage it's almost always one or the other.

MADONNA: Look. Are you going to get those worms you promised to give me?

DOROTHY: You're threatening to walk out?

MADONNA: Yes!

DOROTHY: Madonna, don't you recognize me?

MADONNA: I've never seen you before in my life!

DOROTHY: Right.

MADONNA: Have I?

DOROTHY: You've seen Stevie and John.

MADONNA: What's that got to do with you?

DOROTHY: I'm one of them. The aggressors of the world. While you're a born victim. Like Barney. He didn't walk out either.

MADONNA: Well, I am!

DOROTHY: Madonna! I'll give you the worms!

MADONNA: *Pausing.* When?

DOROTHY: Soon.

MADONNA: Now.

DOROTHY: Soon.

MADONNA: Well. . . .

DOROTHY: Sit down.

MADONNA: You're a strange person.

DOROTHY: Yeah?

MADONNA: Yes. In this business. It seems like an odd one for a woman.

DOROTHY: I think it's great. I'm my own boss.

MADONNA: That must be nice.

DOROTHY: It is.

MADONNA: Don't you mind — touching those things?

DOROTHY: Be tough if I did. It takes about a year and a half for my worms to grow to full size and in that time I have to handle them about thirty or forty times.

MADONNA: Yeech.

DOROTHY: You want to know something that fascinates me about worms?

MADONNA: Not really —

DOROTHY: They're bisexual.

MADONNA: I didn't know that.

DOROTHY: Most people don't.

MADONNA: I guess most people wouldn't even want to.

DOROTHY: They can lay eggs with another worm, understand, but they don't have to. They can do it all by themselves.

MADONNA: Oh.

DOROTHY: Isn't that interesting?

MADONNA: Well. . . .

DOROTHY: Wouldn't it be great if people were that way?

MADONNA: No. You need love.

DOROTHY: Do you, Madonna?

MADONNA: That was an impersonal "you."

DOROTHY: Imagine — if John were a worm he could have had little Stevie all by himself.

MADONNA: But he's not a worm, he's a man. So he needed me.

DOROTHY: Does he need you now?

MADONNA: I'm getting out of here! I don't want to talk to you any more!

DOROTHY: Really?

Madonna crosses quickly to the door, rather apathetically attempts to open it, then turns to Dorothy.

MADONNA: It won't open! You — When did you lock it?

DOROTHY: You weren't trying very hard to open it. Maybe it's just stuck.

MADONNA: I . . . I'm weak.

DOROTHY: With a shape like that? You look to me like a good strong country girl who could do a lot of things.

MADONNA: I know what you want.

DOROTHY: Oh?

MADONNA: Yes. Yes, I've heard all about women like you. I mean, telling me about the sex life of your worms. About how they're — queer.

DOROTHY: Worms are not queer.

MADONNA: They're queer! They're androgynous! You have queer worms here.

DOROTHY: Madonna, that's natural for worms.

MADONNA: You admitted they can get together if they want to! You probably don't let them have anything to do with each other!

DOROTHY: Christ.

MADONNA: You encourage them to do unnatural things!

DOROTHY: You think I go poking around through the dirt after them with a flashlight?

MADONNA: Yes! You do. I bet you watch them.

DOROTHY: *Laughing.* Oh, Madonna. You are something else.

MADONNA: Well, I'm not going to play that game. You're not getting anywhere with me.

DOROTHY: What game do you want to play?

MADONNA: No, sir. No woman is ever going to get fresh with me. That's where I draw the line. You think you're going to get me drunk on that miserable wormy wine and take me to bed. Well, let me tell you a thing or two — I'm not that kind.

DOROTHY: What kind are you?

MADONNA: I like men — that's what I like. John. You should have seen the way I went for him. Oh, yessss. Did I go for him. We used to park . . . down around the other side of the lake. And he'd get me going — that way — and I'd get so carried away I didn't care about anything. Did I feel like a woman then. Umm. I was a woman and I got pregnant and John did finally marry me. . . .

DOROTHY: My, you're enjoying that, aren't you?

MADONNA: No! But — I wanted to tell you.

DOROTHY: You told me. Like for ten minutes.

MADONNA: I was just explaining!

DOROTHY: What game do you want to play, Madonna?

MADONNA: I don't have time to play anything.

DOROTHY: They say that human sperm looks like a tadpole.

MADONNA: Yes. I've heard —

DOROTHY: But I prefer to think of human sperms as worms.

MADONNA: Worms . . .

DOROTHY: Think of that, Madonna. *Madonna slowly moves close to a bin and looks in, seeming hypnotized; Dorothy takes a container of worms from the table and brings it to the bin.* I like to think of that sometimes. You want to see? Look. *She dumps the contents into the bin.* Look at them curl and writhe. Look at that long, fat one — veins and ribs on him. See? How he slides down . . . down . . . there goes the last bit of him. Down . . .

MADONNA: What do you think worm sperm looks like . . .?

DOROTHY: *Abruptly breaking and moving away.* Why do you hate worms?

MADONNA: I never thought about it. . . .

DOROTHY: So think.

MADONNA: I hate worms because. . . .

DOROTHY: Yes?

MADONNA: It was after my mother died. At the cemetery. There was something about the rain that morning . . . as if everything were turned around. As if the wet were oozing from the ground and dropping upward. It was so slow . . . or maybe it just seemed slow to me. But even the trees didn't drip. Instead they seemed to be growing wet strings up from their tops. It was that odd time of year between winter and the first of spring. When the land seems to reject rain. And thinks maybe we'll crawl into buses and leave — a mass exodus. Like lemmings! While the octopus soul of God moves again into all the empty rooms. And that morning — in the rain — I saw the worms. I saw them crawling out of the wet ground as they lowered my mother's coffin. And I knew they were going to crawl inside there with my beautiful mother! She really was beautiful, you know . . . you could see through her skin to the ticking blue veins and they matched her eyes. She wasn't at all like me . . . But that night — the worms — I dreamed about the worms that night! I saw them crawling up the holes of her nose into her head . . . And I thought —I thought she bent over to kiss me — over my bed the way she always did before — and the worms were hanging there — from her nose . . . like boogies . . . hanging there!

DOROTHY: Madonna, you're lying.

MADONNA: No!

DOROTHY: Your mother's a fat woman who lives in Zanesville, Ohio and never writes because she's too busy running the family pizza shop. You used to work there and sprinkle cheese on pizza and one day there were worms in the cheese and you knew it, but you sprinkled it on anyway and cooked the worms under the flame hearing them snap and sizzle. Because your mother was a bitch on wheels and would kill you for wasting cheese.

MADONNA: You don't know me!

DOROTHY: No, I'm guessing.

MADONNA: It was a bad guess.

DOROTHY: Maybe it was. But I had wormy cheese once.

MADONNA: Not these kinds of worms.

DOROTHY: Worms are worms.

MADONNA: Yes. Yes, they are!

DOROTHY: Even the worms people get in their bellies that crawl up in their throats and make them cough.

MADONNA: All right!

DOROTHY: Yes. All right, Mrs. Miller. *Madonna turns to her.* The game ended in a tie.

MADONNA: What game . . .?

DOROTHY: The one we were playing. How many worms do you want?

MADONNA: I'm so tired. . . .

DOROTHY: I'm sorry.

MADONNA: You're not sorry for anything.

DOROTHY: Perhaps —

MADONNA: Anybody —

DOROTHY: Now, Mrs. Miller —

MADONNA: It takes Mrs. Miller all the strength she has every day just to. . . .

DOROTHY: Live.

MADONNA: To face that damn kid.

DOROTHY: Um.

MADONNA: And John.

DOROTHY: I'm asking you, Mrs. Miller. How many — ?

MADONNA: Don't you understand me?

DOROTHY: Yes.

MADONNA: I can't go home. Not right now. Not when I feel this way. They'll . . . they'll trample me underfoot. They do anyway.

DOROTHY: I think you'd better go, Mrs. Miller. Somewhere.

MADONNA: Don't make me! I want to sit here for a little while.

DOROTHY: They'll miss you.

MADONNA: No. They won't.

DOROTHY: Poor Madonna.

MADONNA: The air is strange in here. Damp . . . seeping, earthy smell like the breath of ghosts.

DOROTHY: That's the soil and the spring water I use. Good, cool spring water for my worms.

MADONNA: Don't you hate to sell them? For fishermen to put on hooks?

DOROTHY: No.

MADONNA: Why not?

DOROTHY: I find deaths interesting.

MADONNA: That's cruel.

DOROTHY: Detached.

MADONNA: Nobody's detached from death.

DOROTHY: There is a gentleness in dying.

MADONNA: You never saw anybody you loved die.

DOROTHY: Do husbands count?

MADONNA: Your — Barney?

DOROTHY: I stayed right with him at the end. It was marvelous. He actually changed colors. Just lay there on the white sheet changing colors and moving his fingers a little. His hands were so quiet and almost — transparent while he was sick. And then they started to curl and his thumbs began to move in toward the palms of his hands and his fingers wrapped over them . . . like quiet worms dying.

MADONNA: You're revolting.

DOROTHY: Why? Because I admit things that you only think about?

MADONNA: I'm all heart!

DOROTHY: And sex fantasies.

MADONNA: They're not fantasies! I've had a lot of sex. I'm modern.

DOROTHY: So you dance nude on your stages —

MADONNA: I don't.

DOROTHY: Impersonal "you" again.

MADONNA: And they certainly don't at the summer theatre across the lake. They only do nice comedies there.

DOROTHY: About sex.

MADONNA: Well, of course.

DOROTHY: We've turned the lights on sex.

MADONNA: And it's crawling out of the bins!

DOROTHY: Opposite of the worms.

MADONNA: Naturally.

DOROTHY: Because death still eludes us.

MADONNA: Well, it isn't as interesting.

DOROTHY: Isn't it?

MADONNA: No! You don't want it the way you want sex.

DOROTHY: Why not? It's just as animal and just as primitive.

MADONNA: It's not nice.

DOROTHY: We can't watch it without wincing. We can't die like we make love.

MADONNA: Who'd want to?

DOROTHY: Me, for one.

MADONNA: How dreadful.

DOROTHY: You, for another.

MADONNA: Me? I have a strong will to live!

DOROTHY: Sometimes that's just a death wish in disguise, Madonna.

MADONNA: Do you really think so. . . .?

DOROTHY: Don't you?

MADONNA: I . . . don't know.

DOROTHY: *Stroking her hair from behind.* Think about it.

MADONNA: Ask me. . . .

DOROTHY: Let me. Let me, Madonna.

MADONNA: You asked. . . .

DOROTHY: Do you want to take your worms and go?

MADONNA: The door is locked.

DOROTHY: No, Madonna. It hasn't been locked. It just shuts tight — a good tug can open it any time.

MADONNA: . . . my beautiful mother dropped over dead one morning. It was beside the kitchen range when she was frying an egg. When the undertaker came to the house, I thought he was going to take me away too.

DOROTHY: And you've always been sorry he didn't.

MADONNA: Have I?

DOROTHY: You'd like to be quiet and dead. And beautiful.

MADONNA: Are you beautiful when you're dead?

DOROTHY: Everybody says so.

MADONNA: Yes. At funerals. They do, don't they?

DOROTHY: You always look better after you're dead.

MADONNA: Embalmed. No more dirty finger nails. No more indigestion from onions. Your hair stays curled. Your dress never wrinkles again. There's a soft silk cover —

DOROTHY: — in lavender —

MADONNA: Yes . . . for the cool mornings of forever. You're set. For all time.

DOROTHY: Beautiful.

MADONNA: Yes. . . .

DOROTHY: Madonna, does the war bother you?

MADONNA: Which one?

DOROTHY: Any one.

MADONNA: Oh, yes. All the killing . . . all the bad news . . . all the time. . . .

DOROTHY: I love it, Madonna. I love the dying and the violence.

The living excitement of horror. The final solution of the overcrowd-
ing of the species. But all I ever do is just sit here and listen. Sit with
my worms while it (*Thumping the old radio*) pours out the outra-
geous joy other people are having. Getting my vicarious thrills. But
I'm never a part of it. I always wanted to be a part of it. When are
you more alive than at the moment of sheer horror? *There is a pause
while Madonna looks at her.* Go home, Madonna.

MADONNA: You don't want me to.

DOROTHY: No.

MADONNA: I wasn't sure — when you asked me —

DOROTHY: Don't you want to go now?

MADONNA: No.

DOROTHY: I think you'd better.

MADONNA: No.

DOROTHY: All right.

MADONNA: . . . it's so quiet, isn't it? . . .

DOROTHY: Yes.

MADONNA: I didn't think violence would be this quiet.

DOROTHY: It will get louder.

MADONNA: But then — afterward — it will be quiet again?

DOROTHY: Oh, yes. Very quiet.

MADONNA: Good.

DOROTHY: I'm glad you came.

MADONNA: Just — don't tell me it's beautiful. Don't tell me that. *Dorothy nods, then slowly turns and leaves, firmly closing the door behind her. Madonna looks at the light bulb in the room with fascination, reaching toward it. With her hands outstretched, her thumbs turn inward toward her palm and her fingers close over them. She is looking at her hands almost questioningly when the light goes out. The blackness is complete, intense, and very loud.*

CURTAIN

Manitoba

BY GUY GAUTHIER

> MANITOBA was originally presented by Al Carmines at the Judson Poets Theatre, 55 Washington Square South, in February, 1970. The production was directed by Richard Lipton and featured the following actors:

YO . . . . Art O'Reilly
CHUCK . . . . Cliff De Young
KELLY . . . . Doris Gramovot
PLUMBER . . . . J. P. Paradine
DORIE . . . . Gretchen Oehler
FLET . . . . Richard Pinter
MCALISTER . . . . Barry Kael

Approximate playing time: 30 minutes

A bare stage with two doors and a window. One door leads to the bathroom. The other leads into the kitchen. The stage is in darkness. In the dark, we hear someone playing a recorder softly. When the lights slowly come up, we see Yo lying down on his back playing softly. He has long hair.

After a while, Chuck comes in. He has long curly hair and a beard. Chuck goes into the kitchen. Yo pays no attention to him and keeps on playing. Chuck comes back with a bag of cookies, and a quart of milk and a glass. He sets the milk and cookies down by the window. He looks out of the open window. It is a very hot summer afternoon. They are hot and sweaty. We hear the sound of typing coming from offstage, short, intermittent bursts of typing.

Chuck dunks the cookies in the milk and eats them. He washes them down with milk. After a while he takes a huge mass of loose change out of his pocket. He starts counting the change slowly, while eating the cookies. He piles the quarters in little piles of four, and the dimes and nickels in little piles of five each, to find out exactly how much change he has.

CHUCK: Some cars shouldn't be on the road at all. *A pause.* Would you believe a car with three bald tires on it? Not one, not two. Three! *A pause.* And how about a back door that won't open. *A pause.* And there's a spring sticking out of the back seat. *A long pause.* Did you ever walk out of an air-conditioned building and climb into a cab that's been sitting in the sun? It's like sticking your head into an oven. *Yo pays no attention to him and keeps on playing his recorder. Kelly comes in and goes into the bathroom. Chuck pays no attention to her. We hear the sound of typing coming from offstage.*

CHUCK: Eaton's is the best place to sit. *A pause.* But there's no shade. *A pause.* So you sit there in the sun and you watch the fares come streaming out with parcels and shopping bags. They come out of that air-conditioned building, and when they climb into your cab, they just about faint.

The Plumber comes out of the bathroom with a section of pipe and a big wrench. Now and then, he wipes sweat off his forehead. Yo pays no attention to him and keeps on playing. Neither does Chuck who keeps counting his loose change. We hear the sound of typing coming from offstage.

Al Ingegno

THE PLUMBER: It's all about the Ming dynasty. *A pause.* You know. Rice paddies. Pirates on the Yellow Sea. *A pause.* And the winter monsoon. And the bamboo trees. *A long pause.* Did you know that the Ming dynasty was overthrown by the Manchu dynasty? You didn't know that, did you? *A pause.* And what about the I Ching. And the Lamas. It's fascinating. *A pause.* And just take a look at the pagodas. Like the Great Pagoda of the Wild Geese. You can't beat that. *The Plumber has left the door of the bathroom partly open, and from time to time, he leans over and looks into the bathroom.*

THE PLUMBER: And there's something about Nostradamus and the year two thousand. *A pause.* It's not bad. You should read it.

We hear the sound of typing coming from offstage. Chuck is adding up the many little piles of change.

CHUCK: It's better at night. *A pause.* There's nothing doing, but at least it's cool. *A pause.* You cruise around slowly through the empty streets, listening to your radio. You listen to an old song by the Stones, and in the middle of the song, you hear somebody say, hey, Johnson, you got a trip for me? How about a nice big airport trip? The Stones are singing about some girl, and somebody says, goodnight, gang. It's dead, I'm going home. *A pause.* But it's great when it rains. Things are really jumping when it pours. *A pause.* People run out into the street waving at you, but you drive right by because you've got a fare already.

Chuck picks up the change and puts it into his pocket. He gets up and, taking out his car keys, goes out, leaving behind the cookies and milk.

THE PLUMBER: Ever read Chinese poetry? You should try it. *A pause.* How about that Li Po, eh? Isn't he something? *A pause.* He wrote his best stuff when he was drunk. *A pause.* Maybe that's what it takes. *A pause.* And what about Genghis Khan? You know, the

Mongolian hordes and all that. Now, there's something. *A long pause.* They didn't have tanks in those days.

We hear the sound of the toilet flushing. The Plumber takes a quick look into the bathroom. A moment later, Kelly comes out of the bathroom, fastening up her pants. The Plumber gets up and goes into the bathroom with the wrench and the section of pipe. Yo keeps on playing, paying no attention. We hear the sound of typing coming from offstage. Kelly gets the milk and cookies and starts toward the kitchen. She stops and looks at Yo. She comes over and sits down beside him. Yo keeps on playing.

KELLY: You know what toilets are like. *A pause.* Now and then, you have to clean them, or they turn yellow. *A pause.* Bit by bit, over the months, they turn yellow around the bottom. *A pause.* Because when people take a leak, they forget to flush the toilet. *A pause.* You tell them. You tell them again and again. *A pause.* But they still don't flush it, with the result that the toilet bowl turns yellow. *A pause.* Very yellow. *A pause.* Then it turns brown. *A pause.* And when you don't scrub it out, it gets to the point where you don't want to scrub it out, because you take one look at it, and you decide to put it off till later. *She gets up.* But one of these days . . . *A pause.* Yes, one of these days . . . *Kelly goes into the kitchen with the milk and cookies. Yo keeps on playing. We hear the sound of typing coming from offstage. The typing stops. Yo keeps on playing. Finally, Yo gets up and goes out, taking his recorder with him.*

The stage is now empty. There is a long pause.

Flet comes up to the open window from the outside. He has long hair and wears a thick winter parka. It looks new and the price tag is still on it. He is carrying a pair of snowshoes. They look new and the price tag is still on them. Flet sticks his head in through the window and looks around, with wonder and amazement. Or rather, he sticks his head out and looks around outside, for it now seems that

Flet is inside a building and looking out through the window. Flet squeezes through the window and sits on the ledge. Looking around outside, with the same wonder and amazement as before, he puts on the snowshoes, carefully fastening the straps.

McAlister comes up to the window. He has long hair. He is wearing a thick winter parka and carrying a pair of snowshoes. The parka and the snowshoes look new, and we can still see the price tags on them. Flet steps down from the ledge and walks around, carefully testing his snowshoes. McAlister sticks his head out through the window and looks around, with wonder and amazement. McAlister squeezes through the window and sits on the ledge.

MCALISTER: These parkas are not bad. *A pause.* Mine's a bit big. *A pause.* Too bad I can't exchange it. *He laughs at this.*

McAlister, sitting on the ledge, puts on his snowshoes, but he is having trouble with the straps. Flet walks away, then calls back.

FLET: McAlister! What are you doing? Come on, man. It's beautiful out here.

MACALISTER: I can't get these bloody straps on. *McAlister finally fastens the straps. He steps down from the ledge, and walks around testing his snowshoes carefully.*

FLET: Now, you tell me, did Portage Avenue ever look like this? Did it ever look anything like this? *A pause.*

MCALISTER: One day, that's all it took. One day. *A pause.* And now, it's a clear day again. The sun's shining like nothing had happened. *A pause.*

FLET: Man, that snow is bright. *A pause.*

MCALISTER: Hold it. I've got just the thing. *McAlister searches in his pockets for a moment, then takes out a pair of sunglasses. The little sticker with the price on it is still on the glasses.*

MCALISTER: Courtesy of Eaton's.

FLET: McAlister, you're getting better all the time. I didn't even see you take them. *Flet puts on the sunglasses and looks around.*

FLET: Hey. Green snow. *A pause.* Hey, I'm standing on something hard. *He brushes away the snow under him.* Wow. Look at that! It's a car. That's the top of a car, man.

MCALISTER: Hey, you're right. Some guy's car is down there. *A pause.* You know what? I'll bet we're standing on a whole line of parked cars! I mean, here we are downtown, and there's nothing but snow. They're all down there, man! Cabs, parking meters, mailboxes!

FLET: Yeah, isn't it great? The whole big machine has come grinding to a halt! The schools are closed. The buses are stalled. There's not even any ambulances. They're using helicopters to airlift the patients. The whole city's paralysed! *A pause.* You know, when I came to this town, they told me it would snow a lot. And I've seen blizzards before. But this is something else. I mean, when you step right out of a second story window and go for a walk! *Brushing the snow off his hands, he blows on them to keep them warm.* Hey, we forgot to pick up some gloves. *McAlister digs a pair of gloves out of his pocket. He holds it out to Flet with a smile.*

FLET: McAlister, you're an artist. *Flet puts on the gloves.*

MCALISTER: And that's not all. *He pulls out a pair of nylons.*

FLET: Nylons?

MCALISTER: For the old lady. *A pause.* I've got enough stuff on me to open up a store of my own. *Pulling out a rubber plug for a bath-tub, he looks a bit surprised.* Where did I get this? *A pause.*

FLET: Say, did you see that little snowmobile down there?! Man, what we could do with that snowmobile! I mean, then we could be riding in style! None of this plodding around with snowshoes. *A pause.* McAlister? How about it? You think we can get that thing out here?

MCALISTER: Aw, come on, Flet. We can't just go down there and walk away with a snowmobile!

FLET: McAlister, old pal, I'll pretend I didn't hear that. Don't worry. It won't be a mark on your record.

MCALISTER: Even if we could pull it off, we'd need an elevator to get it up here. And how would we get the fucken thing out of this window?

FLET: But how else can we get around? *A pause.* I want to ride down those streets and see it all. I want to see it with my own eyes! Think of it, every street in the city looks like this. *A pause.* But we'll never get to see it all without a snowmobile.

MCALISTER: But, man, we've got snowshoes. If you want to see the streets, let's just go for a walk.

FLET: Are you sure we can get through that snow? You can barely stay afloat with these things.

MCALISTER: Sure we can. Come on. We'll work up an appetite for dinner.

FLET: I don't need to work up an appetite. I've got one already.

MCALISTER: Come on. We'll walk up to the Bay.

FLET: Hey, that's right. The Bay!

MCALISTER: We'll have a look at the Mall.

FLET: OK. You lead the way. I'm right behind you. *As they walk McAlister takes a roll of Beechnut Menthol cough drops out of his pocket.*

MCALISTER: Here, this ought to hold you till dinner.

FLET: Beechnut Menthol!! McAlister, I love you!

They walk away slowly, plodding through the snow with their snow-shoes.

INTERMISSION

ACT TWO

Flet and McAlister come plodding back, weary and out of breath.

FLET: I don't believe it. There just isn't that much snow in the world. *A pause.*

MCALISTER: You know, a guy could sink out of sight in this stuff.

FLET: Did you see that building on Ellice? The snow went right up to the third floor windows! *A pause.* Say, do you think . . . we could maybe ski down out of one of those windows? Like, I mean, let's make the most of it while it lasts. *A pause.* Didn't we see some skis in there?! *A pause.* So, ah, maybe we should take another swing through the sportswear section. Who knows? Those skis might still be there.

MCALISTER: I don't know, man. We don't want to push our luck. I'm loaded with stuff already. I'd just like to ditch some of it somewhere, before we go back in.

FLET: You're right. We mustn't be greedy. Cause it's got to last. They'll never get all this snow out of here. Never. So we've got to live off these stores for a long time. From now on, we take only what we need. Cause it's got to last us all winter.

The sound of the snow removal machines working in the distance is heard.

FLET: Hey, what's that? Do you hear that?

MCALISTER: Yeah.

FLET: What is it? *A pause.*

MCALISTER: It's the snow machines.

FLET: The snow machines! But it can't be! *A pause* McAlister, they're going to dig us out, they're actually going to dig us out! They want to take away all this beautiful snow!

MCALISTER: Yeah. Looks pretty bad. *A pause.*

FLET: McAlister, what's happening? You said . . . you said there'd be another great Ice Age. You said it would begin right here, here and now. This was the first big push, remember? This was the Return of the Ice Age. That's what you said, man. *A pause* "We're all going to become trappers and live in igloos. We're going to wear sealskin coats and live on whale oil and blubber. And Polar bears will wander in from the North. And everybody will have his own team of huskies. And nobody will need a fridge any more, but frozen foods will still be popular. And there'll always be plenty of ice to put in our drinks."

MCALISTER: Like I said, it doesn't look good. *A pause.* I think it's time to pack it up and get out of here, before the Eaton's people start counting their snowshoes. How about it, Flet? Let's split.

FLET: But we can't leave now! It's almost dinnertime. *A pause.* And besides, we've got another whole day before the snow machines get here.

MCALISTER: I'd rather get this stuff down to my place first.

FLET: But it's almost a mile to your place. We'll never make it. *A pause.* What's come over you, man? You're going to walk out on a free meal? *A pause.* You know what's the trouble with you? You're always hanging around on the first floor. You should spend some time on the fourth floor. All the chicks are up there, hanging around the ladies' wear section. *A pause. Pointing toward the snow machines.* Hey, those guys mean business!

MCALISTER: Looks like we'll have to break the news to them. We'll have to tell them the snow machines are coming.

FLET: Yeah. They'll really take it hard. *McAlister laughs.* No, I mean it! There's two hundred satisfied customers in there. I'm not kidding you, man. Those shoppers are having the time of their lives! They're getting free meals, and sleeping on brand new beds. And Eaton's keeps telling them, we're very sorry, but we can't let you go home just now. It wouldn't be safe. There's still too much snow. But the snow removal machines will be here soon. And they keep smiling at everybody, trying to keep the morale up. They don't seem to realize that morale is great. The shoppers are having a ball. They love every minute of it. They're all getting to know each other. And the guys are hustling the chicks. And you should see the record counter! They're playing all the latest LPs and dancing the night away. I'm telling you, these people don't want to come out. *A pause.* Now, how can a guy walk out on a set up like that? Man, we've never had it so good. *A pause.*

MCALISTER: OK. We'll go in for dinner. But we'll leave this stuff near the window, where we can get it on the way out. I don't want to take it down with us.

FLET: Now you're talking *A pause*. After dinner, I'll get that pair of skis. Then we split, OK? *Listening to the snow machines*. Just listen to that. *A pause*. They're closing in on us, Mac. Time is running out.

Flet climbs back in through the window.

FLET: What are you having for dinner? I'm having cheese-burgers and ice cream. *McAlister climbs back in through the window.*

MCALISTER: I don't know. *A pause*. I think I'll have a Western omelet. *A pause*. With Jello. *They walk away inside the building. The stage is now empty. There is a long pause.*

Yo comes back with a guitar. He settles down on the floor and starts playing chords on his guitar. But the strings are all terribly out of tune and the sound that comes out of the guitar is very strange. But he does not seem to mind this. We hear the sound of typing coming from offstage.

The Plumber comes out of the bathroom and starts packing up his tools. Yo pays no attention to him. He keeps on playing, bringing strange sounds out of his guitar. He stops now and then to tune one of his strings. But he tunes it in such away that all the strings still remain terribly out of tune. He does not seem to mind this.

THE PLUMBER: I think I'll learn Chinese. *A pause*. I'll take a night course. *A pause*. Gotta be ready. *A pause*. You never know when it might come in handy. *A pause*. You know, Chinese cooking is just about the best in the world. *A pause*. I wouldn't mind eating Chinese food all the time. I like chow mein and fried rice.

The Plumber is finished packing his tools. He picks up his toolbox

*and leaves. Yo pays no attention to him and keeps on playing. We
hear the sound of typing offstage. The typing stops, and a moment
later, Dorie comes in. She looks at Yo, stretches and yawns.*

DORIE: There are so many new writers. So many names. *A pause.*
It's make you dizzy. There 's just too much going on.

*She looks out of the open window. It is a very hot summer after-
noon, and she is hot and sweaty.*

DORIE: I guess it's the same in every field. Overproduction. *A pause.*
I read their stuff, and I think, who are all these people?

*Dorie goes into the kitchen. Yo keeps on playing. Dorie comes out
drinking a can of Pepsi. She lights up a cigarette.*

DORIE: It feels funny typing out rejection slips. I don't like it. *A
pause.* We're being swamped with material. I don't know where it's
all coming from. I mean, it's just a little underground magazine.
We can't even pay them. *A pause.* They work hard for months and
months. But me . . . it only takes me acouple of minutes to make
up my mind. All I do is move my hand to the left, toward the pile
of rejects, or I move it to the right, toward the pile of promising
possibilities. That's all, just a little motion to the left or to the right.
What's that to me? And it means so much to them. *A pause.* And
then you read something good and you think, oh, no, don't tell me
he's good! Not another one! Not another promising writer! *A pause.*
It's too much. You can't keep up to it all.

*Yo pays no attention to her. He keeps on playing. Dorie goes out.
Yo keeps tuning the strings of his guitar, but they always remain ter-
ribly out of tune. Kelly comes out of the kitchen. She listens to Yo
playing his guitar. Then she slips a dollar bill into his shirt pocket.*

KELLY: The art of smoking cigarette butts is both delicate and demanding. *A pause.* You grow more desperate with each one you try. *A pause.* As you search through the ashtrays, you find you've already smoked the best ones. The long ones. *A pause.* The trick is to light them without burning the tip of your nose. *A pause.* And then there's the art of smoking them down to the filter without burning your lips. *A pause.* And when you're out of matches, as we most certainly are, then the whole operation becomes even more delicate. I would even say impossible. *A pause.* Of course, there are matches at the store. *A pause.* And cigarettes too. *A pause.* But I wouldn't recommend anything quite so drastic. There are other ways. *A pause.* For instance, I could start rubbing sticks together until I got a flame. *A pause.* All I have to do now is find some sticks.

Kelly goes out. Yo keeps on playing. He sits there alone and keeps on playing strange chords on his guitar. His playing slowly develops into a brilliant performance, a long outburst of fine guitar playing. It is a command performance, so much so that when he is finished, the applause will be for him.

CURTAIN

Set It Down With Gold On Lasting Pillars

BY FREDERICK BAILEY

SET IT DOWN WITH GOLD was originally presented by Shaunee Laurence at the Playbox, 94 St. Marks Place, New York City, in August, 1971. The production was directed by Jack Sims and featured the following actors:

HOWARD . . . . Ross London
INGRID . . . . Mary Anne Schell

Approximately playing time: 7 minutes

A dingy room with a single battered armchair in the center and a clothes tree on the right. An overcoat is hanging on the tree. INGRID *is sitting in the armchair reading a magazine as* HOWARD *enters.*

HOWARD: *with desperation.* My god. My dear god.

INGRID: *with concern.* What is it, Howard?

HOWARD: My god, what are we gonna do?

INGRID: *urgently.* Howard, what is it? *standing.* Tell me what's wrong!

HOWARD: *looks at her.* Ingrid, I— My god! What can we do now?

INGRID: *frantically.* Howard! What's the matter, for garden seed?

HOWARD: Ingrid— *looks down.* Ingrid—

INGRID: Howard?

HOWARD: Ingrid, we— *fearfully.* We're out of peanut butter.

INGRID: *sinking into the nearest chair.* Oh dear Gussie. *A tense moment ensues.* Howard? What will we do, Howard?

HOWARD: *relaxing now that he's confessed.* Don't worry, dear. I'll— *gesturing spastically.* I'll think of something.

INGRID: *getting panicky.* Howard, do you know what this means? Do you know what this means, Howard?

HOWARD: *cool.* Calm down, Ingrid.

INGRID: *standing, near panic.* Do you realize, Howard, what this really means? Do you, Howard?

HOWARD: *calm.* Sit down, dear. I'll think of something.

INGRID: *panicky.* For Pete's sake, do you *know* what this *means,* Howard?

HOWARD: *collected.* Yes, dear. *He pushes her back into the chair.* It means . . . we're out of peanut butter.

INGRID: *dribbling.* You've got to *do* something, Howard! You've *got* to do *something!*

HOWARD: *pacing.* Yes, Ingrid, I'm thinking of something.

INGRID: *wiping off her drool.* What are you going to do, Howard?

HOWARD: *losing his temper.* Ingrid, will you shut up! *Regretting his loss of temper, he collects himself.* I'm sorry. But please, be quiet while I think.

INGRID: *her breath quickening.* Howard— *He silences her with a gesture, then resumes his pacing. Another tense moment ensues.* HOWARD *stops. He looks up.* Howard. What are you going to do, Howard?

HOWARD: *after a brief moment.* Ingrid— Ingrid— Ingrid, I'm gonna . . . gonna . . . get in the car . . . and go to the store . . . and buy some more!

INGRID: *gasps.* Howard! *She rises and puts her hand on his arm.* Howard, I'm going with you.

HOWARD: *quickly.* No! You must stay here! *With determination.* I'll go alone.

HOWARD: This is the way it has to be, Ingrid.

He goes to the right, picking up his coat, and begins to leave. She rushes to him, grabs his coat, tears at it.

INGRID: *near hysteria.* No, Howard! Howard, think of the children! Howard!

HOWARD: *articulately.* I *am* thinking of the children, Ingrid. That's why you must stay.

INGRID: *stopping.* Yes . . . yes, you're right, dear. *Turning away.* But go, quickly! Go! *Tableau. They look at each other. He turns and rushes out. She cries after him.* Howard! Howard, don't leave me!

HOWARD: *off.* It's for the children, Ingrid. The children.

INGRID: *stepping back.* Yes, the children. *Sits, sobs.* Of course, the children. *A pause as she waits for his return. She begins to wring her hands. She begins to snivel.* Howard . . . Howard . . . *She begins to wring her feet.* Howard . . .Oh dear Gussie, Howard . . .! *She is about to wring her neck when* HOWARD *re-enters with a paper sack.* Howard, you got it!

HOWARD: *sadly.* Yes. Yes, Ingrid, I got it.

INGRID: *puzzled.* Howard?

HOWARD: *loudly.* But remember this, Ingrid. *He grabs her by the shoulders.* Always remember, my Ingrid, always remember, and never forget.

INGRID: *devotedly.* Yes, Howard, of course I will.

HOWARD: *turning away.* You must remember.

INGRID: *after a while.* But Howard, what is it? *He almost looks at her, over his shoulder.* Howard, what's the matter? You did get it, didn't you?

HOWARD: Yes. For you I got it.

INGRID: You went to the store and got it?

HOWARD: For you, yes.

INGRID: You went to the store in the car and got it?

HOWARD: *tearfully.* Only for you.

INGRID: Then what's wrong? *Pause.* Howard. Howard, you haven't got it in your hand. What's happened, Howard? It's *not* in your hand! *With agitation.* You're not holding it there in your fist! *They struggle for the sack; it crumples; it's empty.*

HOWARD: *with difficulty.* I . . . I . . . I lost it. *Quickly.* It was stolen!

INGRID: *amazed.* You *lost* it.

HOWARD: *going to her.* Only for you, Ingrid my love, only for you and you alone. *Kneeling.* You, you alone. Only you.

INGRID: *sighs, stiffens up.* Well, Howard. Now that you've botched it, there's only one thing left. The only thing we *can* do now.

HOWARD: *pleading.* What? What, Ingrid? Tell me what we can do now.

INGRID: *rising.* The *only* thing we can do now is . . . to get along without it.

HOWARD: *groveling at her feet.* You're right! Of course! You're absolutely right! Get along without it. That's all we can do now is to get along without.

INGRID: *sternly.* Get on your feet, you fool.

HOWARD: *smartly.* Yes, of course. On my feet, of course.

INGRID: *with authority.* Now go about your business.

HOWARD: *obediently.* Yes, Ingrid. About my business. *He starts to leave. He stops, turns back to her. With a sincerely admiring smile.* Ingrid you're the only one for me. *She raises her head majestically. He pauses, then leaves. She sits regally. He burst into the room again.*

HOWARD: *with desperation.* My god! My dear god!

INGRID: *with concern.* Howard? What is it, Howard?

HOWARD: *shocked, looks at her.* My god.

INGRID: *urgently.* What happened, Howard? Howard?

HOWARD: *in a daze.* My god.

INGRID: *becoming frantic, rising.* Howard, dear?

HOWARD: *catastrophic.* We— Ingrid . . . *agonizing, breathing hard.* Ingrid, we're out of mayonaise!

INGRID: *sinking into the nearest chair.* Oh dear Gussie!!

CURTAIN

The Harrison Progressive School

BY STANLEY NELSON

THE HARRISON PROGRES-SIVE SCHOOL was originally presented by Antoni Bastiano at the Playwrights Workshop Club, 14 Waverly Place, New York City, in October, 1968. The production was directed by Rochelle Kane and featured the following actors:

1ST PERSON . . . . Peter Baline
2ND PERSON . . . . Carol Strauss
3RD PERSON . . . . Karen Carbone
4TH PERSON . . . . Susan Flierl
5TH PERSON . . . . Marty Rosenthal

Approximate playing time: 40 minutes

A bare stage, or, if performed in the round, a raised platform. The five persons are seated with arms and legs crossed. They are dressed sloppily—jeans, flannels, sneakers—and their longish hair is unkempt. Each person has a blanket wrapped around his/her shoulders. The five persons are of various sizes and, presumably, both sexes, but it is rather difficult to tell which are male, female or neuter. Their voices, however, which are of different, distinctive pitches, afford a clue of this rather inconsequential mystery. Throughout the play, the persons must speak as if each word, each syllable is revelatory , as if they are participating in a ritual whose progression is just now unfolding and whose meaning becomes clear only through their participation. In order to accomplish this effect, the actors should be encouraged to give stress to whatever words and phrases appeal to their own interior dynamic—articles, prepositions, normally unstressed syllables—thereby enhancing the sensation of a spontaneous encounter with sound and space.

1ST PERSON: *stands*   I   *sits*

2ND PERSON: *stands*   don't   *sits*

3RD PERSON: *stands*   know   *sits*

4TH PERSON: *stands*   a   *sits*

5TH PERSON: *stands*   BOUT   *sits*

1ST: *stands*   that   *sits.*

The standing and sitting is repeated in the following sequence.

2ND: I

3RD: don't

4TH: KNOW

5TH: a

1ST: bout

2ND: *whispered.* that.

3RD: I

4TH: DON'T

5TH: know?

1ST: a

2ND: bout

3RD: *bored* that.

4TH: I

5TH: YOU

1ST: No

4TH: I

3RD: No

5TH: don't

2ND: Who?

5TH: What?

1ST: When?

2ND: how?

3RD: See

4TH: the

pause; they sit.

5TH: *stands* We were . . .

1, 2, 3, 4: *in a jumble, jumping up and down* Yes! yes! yes! yesyes yesyes!

5TH: . . . talking!

1, 2, 3, 4: *revelation, clap hands, jumping up and down* talking! talking! talking! talking!

5TH: We were talking . . . about the *joints!*

A buzzing among the other four persons; they are disgruntled; they sit down again, arms and legs folded, facing the audience.

5TH: *not giving up* No . . .

1, 2, 3, 4: *vicious, pointing at 5th person* No! No! nonononono*no*!

5TH: . . . we were talking . . .

1, 2, 3, 4: *bored* talking, talking, talking, talking . . .

5TH: . . . about the spaces . . .

1, 2, 3, 4: *querulous* Spaces? the spaces? the spaces? Spaces?

5TH: . . . *between* the joints!

1, 2, 3, 4: *revelation, jumps, shouts, backslaps* the spaces! spaces! joints! the joints! the spacejoints! the jointspaces!

2ND: *pacing, hands behind back, meditative* There was a time . . .

1, 3, 4, 5: time! time! key word! key word!

2ND: *pacing, lecturing* A time when we were talking *nods from the others*

4TH: . . . talking . . . *the others look at him/her disdainfully; he/she shuts up.*

2ND: It would seem logical, therefore and thusly, hither and heretofore, logical, it would seem —

1ST: that we were talking —

1, 2, 4, 5: *forming a circle around 3rd person and pointing accusingly* ABOUT IVAN'S MESSY ROOM!

3RD: *matter-of-fact* But I'm not Ivan *points to 5th person* You are Ivan!

5TH: *laughs* But I can't be Ivan—I don't even smoke!

Others nod and mutter "that's right," "that's right," etc.

1ST: *smiling, conciliatory* We've lost Ivan. *Others beam; they agree; they feel good.*

2ND: All right. Now. We'll start from the beginning. You guys sit down. *They sit.* I'm Little Caeser. I'm the Big Boss from downtown. Look: here's the beginning. Here's how it all started. We'll begin—

4TH: So get to the *point!*

2ND: All right. Here goes. There were three men in a boat. It was a cold night in Siberia. We put more marinara in de marinara sauce. Hey, Butoni!

1, 3, 4, 5: *clapping, in a chant* Hey, Butoni! Hey, Butoni! Hey, Butoni!

2ND: Hey, Butoni! Marinaramarinaradomeprimo!

1, 3, 4, 5: *leaning forward, attentive.* Aaach . . . aaach . . . aaach . . . aaach . . .

2ND: *very assured.* Corresponding to Aries, ergo the id indicates on inky indices . . .

1, 3, 4, 5: *impressed, nodding.* Smart . . . smart . . . bright . . .
smart . . . bright . . .

4TH: *as 2nd person begins "Corresponding," etc., he/she pulls out a
small pad, makes notations and speaks to the audience.* If the clock is
a circle and a hemisphere is two halves of a pumpernickel, then the
only viable conclusion as to time . . . *Drifts into silence, puts pad and
pencil back in pocket.*

2ND: . . . melody lingers on in my itty bitty, making me believe that
we've been talking for exactly *checks wrist, which has no watch* . . .
exactly 42 hours!

*No response from the other persons. Pause, then they again begin
their standing/sitting maneuvers, except for 2nd person, who stands
off to the side.*

1ST: I

3RD: don't

4TH: KNOW

5TH: a

1ST: What?

3RD: When?

4TH: Who?

5TH: the

1ST: so

3RD: of

4TH: it

5TH: oink

1ST: beep

3RD: squoooosh

4TH: squeak

5TH: THAT!

2ND: *still assured*. I'll go further than that. I'm *really* willing to go way out on a limb on this one. I not only know how long we've been talking, I *even* know the goddamn name of this place!

1, 3, 4, 5: *patronizing laughs*. . . . poor thing . . . shouldn't have been let out . . . shame, such lovely parents . . . deep-rooted psychoma . . .

2ND: *musters all of his/her courage*. This is the HAR *chokes up* the HAR . . . the HAR *all choked up, can't continue. 4th person stands, runs over to 2ND person, and begins to play "Charades" by cupping his/her hand over his/her own ear.*

2ND: Sounds like! *4th person nods, then does a charade of putting gasoline into a car.* Err . . . HAR . . . HAR . . . HARGAS! *4th person shakes head.* HARMOBILE! *4th person shakes head; 2nd person makes a great effort,* Err . . . Err HARESSO!

1, 3, 5: *dances, claps, excitement.* HARESSO! HARESSO! HARESSO!

4TH *person shakes his/her head to indicate that this is not the entire answer, then again makes the "sound like" sign.*

2ND: Sounds like! *4th person nods; 2nd person beams proudly; 4th person begins to waddle around the stage, clucking.* Sounds like HEN! Sounds like HEN! 4TH *person nods.* HEN! EN! EN! 4TH *person nods.* HARRESSOEN! HARESSOEN! *4th person shakes head.* HAR . . . I . . . SON! SON!

1, 2, 3, 4, 5: *jubilance, backlaps, dances, claps.* HARRISON! HARRISON! HARRISON! HARRISON!

2ND: *triumphant.* THIS IS THE HARRISON PROGRESSIVE SCHOOL!

1, 3, 4, 5; *perplexed, agitated.* Har? . . . prog? . . . ison? . . . school? . . . ressive?

4TH: *steps forward, confronts 2nd person.* If this is *really* the Harrison Progressive School . . .

2ND: I said it: THIS IS THE HARRISON PROGRESSIVE SCHOOL!

4TH: Well, if this is really and truly —

2ND: This is THE HARRISON PROGRESSIVE SCHOOL sure as my name is Misterdashmissusmxtplx!

1ST: All right, fella; answer this one: if this is really THE HARRISON PROGRESSIVE SCHOOL, then what are five of the most important people in the world doing here?

2ND: *still assured.* I've been trying to tell you that we've been here for exactly 42 hours, at THE HARRISON PROGRESSIVE SCHOOL, discussing

1, 2, 4, 5: *quickly forming a circle around 3rd person and pointing accusingly.* IVAN'S MESSY ROOM!

3RD: *laughing.* But I'm *not* Ivan; I've already told you that.

1, 2, 4, 5: *cajoling.* Come on . . . be Ivan . . . You could be Ivan . . . Why not Ivan?

2ND: *settling the matter.* We've been here 42 hours, discussing IVAN'S MESSY ROOM, and we just can't *moving offstage* continue unless one of us, somebody, anybody *reappearing with a wicker chair* takes the place of Ivan, who is lost! *Motions 3rd person to sit; 3rd person sits.* Ivan?

3RD: *to 2nd person.* Yes teacher —

2ND: *agitated.* But I'm not . . .

1, 4, 5: *pointing.* Yes . . . yes you are . . . you are . . . *chanting, clapping, stomping.* YOU'RE THE TEACHER! YOU'RE THE TEACHER! YOU'RE THE TEACHER!

2ND: *more agitated.* I *can't* be the teacher; I *know* too much . . .

1, 4, 5: *chanting louder.* YOU'RE THE TEACHER! YOU'RE THE TEACHER! YOU'RE THE TEACHER!

4th person runs offstage; returns quickly with another wicker chair; 1, 4, 5 point to the chair.

2ND: *sitting, visibly attempting to calm his/her agitation.* Ivan, why is your room messy?

Stage darkens; spots on 2 and 3; 1, 4, 5 move back into the darkness.

3RD: Well, you know, I'm in charge of the nature hut here at THE HARRISON PROGRESSIVE SCHOOL and —

1, 4, 5: *whispered, unseen.* . . . logical . . . logical . . . makes sense . . . makes sense . . . good head on that one . . .

Al Ingegno

3RD: . . . the other day —

2ND: What day? How long?

3RD: Exactly 42 hours —

1, 4, 5: *impressed, whispered, unseen.* . . . right again . . . right again
. . . smart head . . . go places . . . smart head . . .

3RD: . . . 42 hours ago, I was in the nature but for the very last time
of my life —

2ND: How do you know that?

3RD: *ignores question* . . . the very last time. I locked up the rats
and marmosets, tip-toed across the floor, bolted the gate, and, walk-
ing back to my room under the flourescent lights, I thought of
philosophical things —

2ND: Like what?

3RD: Like three men in a cold boat in Siberia. *2nd person nods.* Like
what happens to whipped marinara sauce. Like being pulverized into
the smallest, most indiscernible particle in the universe.

2ND: You're doing well, Ivan. You're explaining it very well. You're
really telling us why your room is messy, why yours is the only messy
room at THE HARRISON PROGRESSIVE SCHOOL.

3RD: Well, you just won't believe what happened next.

2ND: Out with it!

3RD: I saw a tree.

1, 4, 5: *laughing deliriously, still unseen.* Tree . . . tree? . . . flipped,

FLIPPED! . . . off with Ivan's head . . . unsalvageable . . . positively unsalvageable . . .

2ND: *turning head toward* 1, 4, 5. BE QUIET BACK THERE!

1, 4, 5: *offended*. What? . . . what? . . . why the nerve . . . the gall . . .

2ND: I'M THE TEACHER! YOU'LL SPEAK WHEN SPOKEN TO, NOT BEFORE! *Silence, pause.* Ivan, that's a lie, you've never seen a tree in your whole life.

3RD: *like an offended child*. Yes I did! Yes I did!

2ND: *quietly*. No, Ivan—you did *not* see a tree; that's quite impossible. Do you know why?

3RD: *crying*. Why? Why, teacher, why?

2ND: Because trees are outlawed at THE HARRISON PROGRES-SIVE SCHOOL. We don't say "tree." We don't think "tree."

3RD: *still crying*. But if I saw —

2ND: *firm*. That's enough, Ivan. Please continue your explanation, but be sure to tell the truth or you'll be punished.

3RD: *in bits and pieces*. Well . . . in the hut . . .

2ND: Which hut? The dormitory hut? The arts and crafts hut?

3RD: . . . the nature hut . . . on the floor . . .

2ND: What is the floor made of, Ivan?

3RD: . . . the artificial plutonium floor . . . it's made of plutonium planks . . . but there are spaces . . . beautiful spaces . . . cracks in the floor . . . between the planks . . . I can look through . . . I can see gr . . .

2ND: *standing.* DON'T SAY IT, IVAN! IT'S THE SAME AS TREE! WE HAVE EXHAUSTED THE SUBJECT OF THE JOINTS AND SPACES AND CRACKS ON THE FLOOR OF THE NATURE HUT AT THE HARRISON PROGRESSIVE SCHOOL!

3RD: Well . . . can I talk about the ceiling?

2ND: Only if it is pertinent to Ivan's messy room!

3RD: *points to himself.* Me? *2nd person nods.* I'm still Ivan? *2nd person nods.* Okay: the ceiling of the nature hut, which is constructed entirely of uncreased sheet metal ultimately processed at the Keystone Tool and Die Company, 1123 Bouillon Avenue, Franklin Lakes, New Jersey —

2ND: *sighs.* It's out of my hands; Ivan has chosen the path of sacrifice.

3RD: *now completely in his own world.* . . . white . . . whiter . . . whitest . . . *shuts eyes* . . . dark . . . darker . . . darkest . . . deepest . . . lightest . . . in my brain . . . my blood . . . my vulvpenis . . . *face becomes beatific.* . . . I enter . . . I open a door . . . window . . . open . . . I can breathe . . . air . . . light . . . space . . . a vastness of sky, like when I was young, I lay down in the grass, at night, under a tree, and looked up, in perfect silence, at the stars . . . light . . . lighter . . . light . . .

2ND: *stands, pulls out a rolled up sheet of stiff white paper, unfurls it and reads.* Through the authority vested in me by Englefart Plutonium Limited, the Society for the Eradication of Natural Objects, and THE HARRISON PROGRESSIVE SCHOOL, I hereby sentence you to absolute communication with anathemetized excommunicants and other low persons . . .

1, 4, 5: *as the lights burst on, they surround 2nd person; they are obviously hostile and about to become violent.* KILL THE TEACHER! KILL THE TEACHER! KILL THE TEACHER!

2ND: *backing up toward right exit.* But I'm not the teacher . . . it was pretend . . . you told me to be a pretend teacher . . .

1, 4, 5: *following, stalking.* YOU'RE THE TEACHER! HEY BUTONI! MARINARAMARINARADOMEPRIMO!

2ND: *breaking down, crying, falling to his/her knees.* O God! O God! Forgive me! Have mercy!

1, 4, 5: *dragging 2nd person offstage.* HEY TEACHER! HEY TEACHER! HEY TEACHER!

Offstage, 1, 4, 5 continue their chant of HEY TEACHER! KILL TEACHER! HEY TEACHER!; 2nd person frantically cries out "O God!" "O God!" "O God!"; there is a long piercing scream, then complete silence.

3RD: *adjusting his/her blanket, assuming sitting pose, and addressing audience.* I don't know why they want to punish me. Why is that so important? Why is it so important? I was telling them things; important things. It was all for their own good—don't you agree? I mean, if you see things, then you say things; if you hear things, then you see things; if you say things, then you touch things—and so on. It's a logical progression. They're all for logic—had you noticed? They have no illusions left—no gloss—right down to the very barest of essentials. That's life: THE HARRISON PROGRESSIVE SCHOOL. Three men in a boat; boat begins to leak; only room for two to bail; captain gets up and says —

1, 4, 5: *rushing back onstage, encircling 3rd person.* KILL TEACHER! KILL TEACHER! HEY TEACHER!

3RD: *resigned to his/her fate.* But I'm not the teacher. You just now —this very second—*to audience* Won't you back me up, won't you defend me?—*to 1, 4, 5* You just killed the teacher: don't you remember?

4TH: *pointing, accusing.* You . . . were talking . . . to . . . PEOPLE!

1, 5: *with repugnance.* PEOPLE! AACH! AACH! PEOPLE!

4TH: *vicious.* You're . . . the . . . TEACHER!

3RD: *standing.* No, that's quite impossible, if you'll just consider —

4 stuffs a gag in 3rd person's mouth; 1 and 5 drag 3 off the stage and into an aisle and throw 3 violently to the floor, where he/she remains, face down, throughout the rest of the play. 1, 4, 5, somewhat wearied by their efforts, adjust their blankets and slowly resume their ritual sitting/standing maneuver. Each voice must now be quite distinctive, each syllable spoken like an individual unit of sound. As they speak, they eye each other suspiciously.

1ST: I

4TH: DON'T

5TH: know

1ST: a

4TH: bout

5TH: THAT!

1ST: Don't

4TH: I

5TH: bout

1ST: that

4TH: a

5TH: squeeesh

1ST: who?

4TH: where?

5TH: blat

1ST: frunk

4TH: why?

5TH: why?

1ST: why?

4TH: shlurp.

5TH: shlunk

1, 4: *circling 5th person, menacing.* Shlunk? . . . Shlunk? . . . What shlunk? . . . Where shlunk? . . .

5TH: *backing up, smiling.* Everything is copasetic, fellas . . .

1, 4: *shouting directly in 5's ear.* SHLUNK! SHLUNK! SHLUNK! SHLUNK!

5TH: *backed up against a wall.* But I've always been good . . . I do the right thing . . . I'm one of the good guys, the unbeatables . . . I play with peers and siblings . . .

1, 4: *screaming into 5's face at the top of their lungs.* SHLUNK, SHLUNK! SHLUNK! SHLUNK! SHLUNK!

5TH: *slipping to the floor, crying, covering his/her ears with his/her arms.* . . . blat . . . frunk . . . squeeesh . . .

1, 4: *bending down and whispering into 5's ears as 5 jabbers his/her nonsense syllables.* Shlunk baby . . . Shlunk sweetheart . . . Shlunk baby . . . Shlunk baby . . .

4TH: *standing.* Death is too good for this person.

1ST: *standing.* Yes: this person must be subjected to another final solution.

1 and 4 lift 5th person to his/her feet; 1 violently pulls off 5's blanket and flings it to the front of the stage; 5's shirt is open, revealing that he/she is androgynous: a breast on one side of the chest, thick hair on the other side. 5 covers the one breast with both arms and runs off-stage left, babbling and wild-eyed.

1ST: *brushing his/her hands.* That's that.

4TH: *brushing his/her hands.* Good job.

1ST: THE HARRISON PROG

4TH: GRESSIVE SCHOOL does not tolerate

1, 4: SHLUNKS!

They meticulously adjust their blankets, then assume the sitting position, ready to re-enact the ritual. 1st person begins to stand, but stops halfway, transfixed, unable to utter a sound; then sits. 1 and 4 repeat this maneuver several times, with increasing rapidity; they eye each other suspiciously. Finally, they begin the maneuver simultaneously, but are again transfixed halfway up, unable to complete the action. They turn toward each other briefly, gazing with extreme hostility and suspicion, then race off the stage at opposite exits. They reappear simultaneously, meeting at centerstage. Each now wears a Mexican hat and thrusts a long switchblade at the other's throat.

4TH: *with a Mexican accent.* So compadre: you theenk I fall for your lousee scheeme? You theenk I go to sleep and then you sleet my throat? *laughs deliriously.* Hahahahahaha! Theenk again, compadre, theenk again!

1ST: *with a Mexican accent.* Theenk you, compadre! *laughs deliriously.* Hahahahahaha!

VOICE OFFSTAGE: Hey, Butoni!

1ST: Lousy fall you sleep theenking scheeme? Throat sleet in dee meedle of dee night? Never, babee, never!

In unison, they walk to the back of the stage and sit down against the wall, several yards apart. They arrange their blankets, pull their hats over their eyes, droop their heads on their chests and fold their arms, their switchblades pointed upward. Colored lights burst on and off, creating a prismatic, solar effect; these bursts alternate with brief periods of total darkness. The effect should be one of a concentrated period of time in which the sun is rapidly rising and setting. Even though the sequence lasts only a few minutes, the audience must be aware that a somewhat lengthy period of time has elapsed. Appropriate music can enhance this effect. As the stage lights are turned on again, 4th person leaps to his/her feet and tip-toes stealthily toward 1st person, the switchblade ready for action.

1ST: *leaping to his/her feet, laughing.* Hahahahahaha! What you theenk, bebee? Never I sleep while your shadow is walkeeing dee face of dee earth. I am tuned een on you, compadre; do not geeve me temptation. *They place the switchblades at each other's throats.*

4TH: Lousy reenger! Man of la mancha! I vitelloni, butoni, weel sleet you in your sleep!

In precise unison, they turn away from each other, take a few steps, then wheel around with the switchblades ready; they repeat this maneuver several times until they are at opposite ends of the stage. Then, as if at a specific signal, they race across the stage and drive the switchblades into each other's stomachs. Still in unison, they stagger backwards, then fall on their backs, arms spread, motionless. The lights dim; there is a short pause. Offstage are heard what appear to be five different voices, the distinctive voices of the five persons.

squeeesh

oink

beep

blat

frunk

Another short pause; then 5th person wanders on from the left, still wild-eyed and covering his/her single breast with both arms. 5 steps over a body (1 or 4), walks to the front of the stage, picks up his/her blanket, wraps it around his/her body and assumes the ritual sitting position at centerstage. Then 5 proceeds with the ritual, standing and sitting, speaking in five different voices, the distinctive voices of the five persons.

I

don't

know

a

BOUT

that!

I

don't

KNOW

a

bout

whispered that.

I

DON'T

know?

As 5 repeats the identical phrases spoken at the opening of the play, his/her voices become fainter and fainter and finally die away; the lights grow dimmer as the curtain falls.

CURTAIN

Concentric Circles

BY BENJAMIN BRADFORD

CONCENTRIC CIRCLES was originally presented by Norman Hartman at the Old Reliable Theatre Tavern, 231 East 3rd Street, in January, 1970. The production was directed by Bill Lentsh and featured the following actors:

ALTHEA PERGINE . . . . Maryellen Flynn
LILY PERGINE . . . . Evelyn Jones
CLOVIS MITCHELL . . . . Al Cohen

Approximate playing time: 40 minutes

The curtain opens slowly. It is dusk, the lights have not been turned on. Dimly lighted, an interior is seen. There is a large bow window rear center that is raised one step. The furnishings are Edwardian preserved in Formalin. There are heavy drapes at the window. To right of the bow is a tall oak mirror on a small platform, to the left is a heavy oak chest. There is a door to an entrance hall, stage right, and a door to the dining room, stage left. Downstage right is a library table heavy with books and old papers. There is a day bed stage left, the head raised a little, with a small table nearby. Near the foot of the day bed is a small chair.

The bow of the window is deep and holds a tall needlepoint screen with an almost completed classical scene. There is a small chair near-

*by and another small chair at the far left edge of the bow. Right
of the center downstage is a wheelchair, tall, solid, and wooden.*
ALTHEA PERGANDE *sits quietly in the chair waiting. She wheels herself to the hall door.*

ALTHEA: *cross and loud.* Lillie! *There is no answer.* What are you
doing, Lillie? *She waits a moment and wheels herself center.* Dark!
Disgruntled. It's pitch dark in here. *Quietly.* You know how I hate
the dark. It's one of your gestures, isn't it, to let it get dark . . . and
leave me sitting here in it. *A door is heard opening and closing.* Lillie?

LILLIE: *wearily.* Yes, Althea. *She remains off stage a moment.*

ALTHEA: What are you doing? *She is exasperated. The day has been
long.*

LILLIE: *Appearing in the hall door. She is a very old woman, dressed
in a dark crepe dress hanging loosely to her ankles. The years are
heavy on her shoulders. She is two or three years older than* ALTHEA.
What?

ALTHEA: *louder.* What were you doing? ALTHEA *keeps her back to*
LILLIE.

LILLIE: You know very well what I was doing. *She crosses down.*

ALTHEA: It takes an hour to get the paper?

LILLIE: *handling her the afternoon paper and crossing left.* I was
sitting . . . sitting for a while on the front stoop by the fence watching
the sun set on the marigolds.

ALTHEA: *to the world at large.* Sitting on the stoop, watching the
marigolds. And what is Althea doing? Sitting . . . in the pitch dark.
Turning to LILLIE. I don't expect you to care about that, about me.
I've lived long enough with you . . . *alone* . . . to not expect any-

thing more than what I can do for myself which is precious small thanks to you. You did it to me . . . crippled me. *Turning from her.* Why, I'd be married now, grandchildren all around this house if you hadn't brought me the disease. You brought it home, but it didn't cripple you. LILLIE *has crossed up to the bow window and is peering out the window, oblivious.* You had it, you got up and walked away. But you ruined *my* life, my whole life. You . . . you're not even listening. *Wheeling herself to the step of the window.* What are you doing? Do you think you're young enough to be free?

LILLIE: No. *With resignation.* Not young enough to be anything.

ALTHEA: *haughtily.* Would you mind turning on the lights? I've spent enough time in darkness. I want to read the obituaries. I want to see who died. LILLIE *crosses to center and pulls the light cord, the stage is filled with a soft light.* The paper's dirty. You know I don't like for the paper to be dirty. Did the boy throw it in the mud or did your shaky old hands drop it there? *She abruptly wheels back center.* Sister Lillie, hands aflutter, drops the paper and the butter, drops the eggs and breaks a dozen . . . What rhymes with a dozen? *Casually opening the paper.* Thank goodness the death notices are clean. *She begins to read.*

LILLIE: *hesitantly.* While I was outside Mrs. Grim walked by. She's older than I am and she was smiling. *Crossing to the chair at the foot of the day bed.* What's she got to smile about? *Sitting.* I haven't smiled in days or months, I don't know which. Who's gone? *There is no answer.* Althea, who's dead we know?

ALTHEA: No one. I don't know a soul listed here. They're all . . . younger. Funerals: Harry Keith, age sixty-four, 268 Good Sheppard Street, died at 3:30 A.M. *Looking up.* What a terrible time to die! Imagine dying at 3:30 in the morning. What a bother it must have been. *Back to the paper.* At home. Survived by his wife, four daughters, son, three sisters and two brothers. Funeral services will be held . . .

LILLIE: Did we know him?

ALTHEA: Of course not. He was of a different generation.

LILLIE: Any others?

ALTHEA: A page full.

LILLIE: Anyone . . .

ALTHEA: No. No one you knew. *An edge of triumph.* We've outlived them all. William, Genevieve, and Granny Hobson, all dead and down the drain . . . *Painfully.* And here we sit. *A pause.* A foolish girls was sister Lillie. Now she's sick, senile, and silly . . . that was an onomatopoeia.

LILLIE: Alliteration.

ALTHEA: Onomatopoeia.

LILLIE: Alliteration. *Standing.* I was the teacher, remember?

ALTHEA: And somehow got the idea that teachers knew everything. Teaching didn't do a thing for your personality, my dear. It made you into a bigot and a bore. *Superciliously.* Forgive me. You may have been a bore and a bigot before you taught. I don't remember, it was so long ago.

LILLIE: Would you like the dictionary? I'll bring it to you. *Moving right to the table.*

ALTHEA: I've lost interest in figures of speech.

LILLIE: *seaching about the library table.* I don't think so easily.

ALTHEA: *pouting.* I'd like some water. I'm thirsty.

LILLIE: Wait a minute!

ALTHEA: *louder.* I don't want to wait a minute. I'm thirsty. All my life . . . all my life I have waited for minutes . . .

LILLIE: *Picking up a frayed book.* Here it is. *A step toward* ALTHEA.

ALTHEA: *waving it away.* Put it down and bring me a glass of water.

LILLIE: Because you know you're wrong. *Rifling through the A's.* A . . . L . . . L . . .

ALTHEA: *crossly.* I have no interest in it.

LILLIE: Here it is. *Crossing to* ALTHEA, *putting it before her eyes.* Read it.

ALTHEA: *turning her head.* I said I have no interest in it. *Wheeling a few feet away.* I am interested in my *needs* being met. I am interested in not being constantly irritated by you, by your sense of definition. I am interested in living somewhere in another place with other people. *Wheeling her chair center.* I am interested in comfort. I am interested in movement . . . clouds on a windy day. I am interested in . . .

LILLIE: I am interested in your acknowledging the fact that you are dead wrong. I want . . .

ALTHEA: I am interested by transfiguration . . . *A pause.* The past.

LILLIE: Irrevocable!

ALTHEA: Yes, I know. *Returning to the paper.* And when do I get the water? *The bravura actress.* I am perishing in a Sahara, ah, an oasis yonder. Seen plainly, not an illusion. And I could have made it, had I not been crippled by my sister at an early age. Piteously looking at my withered limbs . . . *Her head falls.* I die. LILLIE *replaces the book on the library table and crosses to the dining room door, left.* Where are you going?

LILLIE: *Flatly.* To get the water. *She exits.*

ALTHEA: *calling after her.* Cold, but not too cold. No ice. Cold enough to frost the glass. And I think I'd like the cranberry glass this time. I like little changes. *Reading the paper to herself.* We did know her, but not well . . . great-grandchildren, and so many. Some people multiply like rabbits. No sense of decency. *Looking up.* Would you hurry? *Again to herself.* Even proud of it. As if procreation implied sensuality. LILLIE *enters carrying the cranberry glass upon a tray.*

LILLIE: *apologetically.* It seems . . . *Offers the tray.*

ALTHEA: *Drawing herself up, horrified.* There is ice in that water. *She does not touch it.*

LILLIE: *continuing* . . . that there is no cold water in the pitcher.

ALTHEA: *furious.* You know I hate ice in water. You did it on purpose . . . I won't drink it. I will not drink water with ice in it.

LILLIE: Yesterday you wouldn't . . .

ALTHEA: I do not admire stagnation. I like changes. I told you clearly, concisely that I did not want water with ice. I absolutely will not drink it. I will die before I will touch that water. You may take it back into the kitchen and you may pour it out. *Wheeling right.* How the privileged punish the unprivileged . . . I am waiting for an apology . . . a sign of contrition . . . LILLIE *crosses up and center, placing the tray upon the chest upstage left.* It there no contrition? . . . apparently none. LILLIE *begins to work on the needle-point.* I could wish that you did not have to help me, service me so to speak. But as you recall, the ability to care for myself was lost a long time ago. Thanks to you and your disease that hobbled me as a young girl, a pretty, running girl, flaxen hair blowing behind me, running down the streets, around the house . . . never still. Men watched me run. And I watched them watch me run. And you watched them watching me. And for a birthday gift you brought me poliomyelitis. Poliomyelitis. *Softly.* Poliomyelitis. What a pretty word for shrunken legs that never ran again. There's a vaccine now. Little girls running in the streets won't have to beg . . . humble mendicants . . . for a glass of water.

LILLIE: *tersely.* I told you I saw Mrs. Grim in the street. She spoke. She said, "hello, Miss Pergande." And I said, "hello, Mrs. Grim."

ALTHEA: What a fascinating thing to hear.

LILLIE: She asked me to a revival, a tent revival in that big field at the end of the street.

ALTHEA: Interesting, interesting.

LILLIE: And she smiled, imagine, as old as she is, she smiled. She said the preaching had made her young again. Young in soul.

ALTHEA: No doubt they brought the fountain of youth along.

LILLIE: *still working at the needlepoint.* I wanted to go.

ALTHEA: *shocked.* You wanted to go?

LILLIE: Yes. I wanted to see what is was about. I wanted something to look forward to.

ALTHEA: You haven't been out of the house except to get my paper in two years.

LILLIE: *persistantly.* I wanted to go. I wanted to smile again.

ALTHEA: What you mean is you wanted to leave me.

LILLIE: To anticipate something. To feel that there is a world outside this house.

ALTHEA: *scornfully.* This house *is* the world. My world because I can't go beyond the door. You world because you made me as I am. *Turning away from* LILLIE. Why don't you go? *A sly look.*

LILLIE: *Carefully.* I'm afraid.

ALTHEA: Of whom, of what? *Wheeling rapidly back to her.* Of people laughing at your shaky, bony old hands, and your head bobbing side to side. *Laughing* You get that here, darling. I laugh at you all the time. Of the miracle that won't work for you. I envision it. Lillie Pergande, stooped and slow, walking, indeed she can still walk, down the aisle to the miracle of youthful salvation. Young again, indeed. *Furiously.* Anticipation goes with the color of the hair, the elasticity of the skin. It doesn't come back . . . it never comes back.

LILLIE: *she affects not to hear most of* ALTHEA *words.* Perhaps that's what I'm afraid of.

ALTHEA: *Smugly.* Besides I already knew about it. It was in the paper. Near the funeral notices. I'm sorry you can't read the paper this week. You know why! And because of the ice in the water you can't read it next week either.

LILLIE: *with futility.* Or the week after or the week after or the week after because of dust on a plate, or waking up too late, or reasons too . . .

ALTHEA: It is my paper.

LILLIE: I know.

ALTHEA: My paper because I buy it. I have the right to share my things when I wish. I am happy to share with you when you have proved yourself to deserve.

LILLIE: It doesn't matter, Althea, doesn't matter anymore. I just thought again of anticipation.

ALTHEA: Gone.

LILLIE: I know, I should have known . . .

ALTHEA: And salvation is gone as well. There is a reason for us to be here, our parent's house, old and gone dry. The shadows of years pausing in a space. There is a reason. Sin and punishment predestined. The only thing you can anticipate is dying.

LILLIE: I thought maybe . . .

ALTHEA: That you could anticipate joy.

LILLIE: A little joy.

ALTHEA: No. Only dying.

LILLIE: There are things worse than dying. Living can be worse than dying. Living with pain, living without joy, living without the expectation of . . .

ALTHEA: Anything except dying. That's all you can look forward to. *Smugly.* I can look forward to the paper every day. I can know what's going on out there. Even with you dirtying the paper I still know. So . . . we take the days and weeks and times that run together and make a life.

LILLIE: *crossing to the chest upstage left.* Would you like the water now? The ice is gone.

ALTHEA: Bring it here. I'll try it. LILLIE *brings her the glass.* The glass is frosted, but it has run, the frosting. *Tasting.* I'll do. I'll drink it. It's not right, but I'll drink it.

LILLIE: Thank you.

ALTHEA: You're welcome. Ah, you see . . . there is politeness left in this house. Two well bred ladies, spinsters, living a life together . . . We may not always say please, but we can say thank you.

LILLIE: And you're welcome.

ALTHEA: *lighter*. Mother would be proud to see her daughters. If Gen hadn't died what fun we might have had.

LILLIE: And William.

ALTHEA: *shaking her head*. William wouldn't have adjusted. It's as well. But Genevieve . . . which part would she have wanted?

LILLIE: She's been dead thirty years, and William forty. I can't know what they'd want today.

ALTHEA: Well, I can. People don't change as they grow older, they simply fix. The submissive stay submissive, and the strong grow stronger. It's just that simple. There is less complexity of character than people think.

LILLIE: They've been gone so long, I don't think I would know either of them if they walked into this room tonight. Do you? *She walks down to the center chair.*

ALTHEA: If they walked into this room tonight in the form in which they died or as they would be twenty, thirty years older? Which? *Wheeling her chair to sit by* LILLIE.

LILLIE: I'm not sure I'd remember them either way.

ALTHEA: Of course I'm younger than you. My memory is better.

LILLIE: I remember many things.

ALTHEA: All inconsequential. As the time of age falls across our backs the one thing we cannot bear is change of role. That's because we've learned it well and long. The only truly unbearable factor . . . not dying, that's bearable . . . is to change position. Don't you think?

LILLIE: *turning away*. I don't think I think anymore.

ALTHEA: No, you don't. But then you never did.

LILLIE: *defensively*. But I taught school all those years.

ALTHEA: *lightly*. Whatever gave you the idea that teachers think? The only thinkers are creative people. Artists . . . Poets . . . Mostly poets. They never stop thinking.

LILLIE: *petulantly*. Teachers do think.

ALTHEA: They do not, they parrot. Polly, pretty polly. You've been a dun colored parrot for eighty years.

LILLIE: Stop . . .

ALTHEA: With a mauve tail and eyes of no color, like a turtle. Sister Lillie, flat and bent, head awobble without intent.

LILLIE: *loudy*. I can't bear your horrible poems.

ALTHEA: Nonsense, it's the fear of my kindness that terrifies you.

LILLIE: Stop. *She runs across the room right and puts her fingers to her ears.* ALTHEA *follows quickly.* LILLIE *walks as fast as she can to the left door.* I'll walk out of this room.

ALTHEA: *laughing*. No, you won't.

LILLIE: I will, I will, I will.

ALTHEA: *laughing loudly.* You won't, you won't, you won't.

LILLIE: Stop it, Althea. I can't bear this game again.

ALTHEA: You can, you can. Bear, bear. Sister Lillie.

LILLIE: *with as much violence as she is capable of.* I said to stop it. *She crosses quickly to the day bed and sits,* ALTHEA *right behind her.*

ALTHEA: Sister Lillie, was a teacher, mimicking another teacher, mimicking another. Knowledge standing, couldn't reach it. But ever, ever could she teach it.

LILLIE: *pleading.* I can't stand it tonight. Not tonight.

ALTHEA: Same as last night and tomorrow night.

LILLIE: Please, Althea, not tonight. Mrs. Grim . . . anticipation . . . please . . .

ALTHEA: Lillie, sister . . .

LILLIE: *her lips pursed.* I'm going to be angry.

ALTHEA: *playfully.* How frightened I am! Sister Lillie found her stage, played her role and not so badly. Until she tried to change the play. Sad, sadder, saddest, sadly. *Shaking her head.* That wasn't very good. Requires refinement. What do you think, Lillie?

LILLIE: If insanity was possible for me. If I could go quickly, quietly mad . . .

ALTHEA: Pergande's don't go mad. They die, but never go mad.

LILLIE: Your poetry . . .

ALTHEA: Is not always perfect. I said the last was not so good. You heard me say. I am not the kind of artist who thinks everything I do is perfect. Now listen quietly, I've been working on this all day.

LILLIE: I won't.

ALTHEA: You will, because you have no choice.

LILLIE: I do have a choice. We all have choices.

ALTHEA: No. There is a time in life when we lose that. And we both lost ours a long time ago. LILLIE *puts her hands to her ears again.* Take your hands down, I'd hate you to miss this. I've worked so hard. *Firmly.* I said take your hands down.

LILLIE: *whimpering.* No . . . no . . .

ALTHEA: *with some gentleness.* Yes. Take your hands from your ears. I do not wish to yell. I do not wish to stress my voice. When Sappho sings the world must listen. And you're the only audience . . . *Turning.* Very well, you cannot deafen yourself forever. And I have enormous patience. What an actress I would have been. If I had had the chance. But I didn't. *Wheeling back to* LILLIE. You are going to listen and you are going to listen now. *Shouting.* Unplug your ears. You *will* hear me.

LILLIE: Not now, I can't now. Not tonight.

ALTHEA: *viciously.* I'm sick of you now. I have spent the better piece of the day thinking. I am never silent in my mind. I have worked and you will hear me. Because it is a masterpiece of poetry. LILLIE *begins to cry softly, she drops her hands from her ears.* Carefully listen, now. LILLIE *stares at her.* Let us make an illusion, you and I, that we have sometime loved each other, that we have felt . . . *The doorbell rings* . . . affection.

LILLIE: *rising.* The doorbell.

ALTHEA: *worried.* I heard it. I haven't heard the doorbell ring after dark in a decade.

LILLIE: No one ever rings our doorbell after dark.

ALTHEA: I know. . . . Answer it.

LILLIE: I'm afraid.

ALTHEA: *a threat.* Answer it.

LILLIE: I'm afraid.

ALTHEA: Of what? What can be done that would impair us? Nothing. Of course you don't know it, but there is nothing in this world or any world for us to fear. Go to the door. LILLIE *takes a hesitant step toward the hall door.* Go on! Whoever it is may go away. I'd hate that. LILLIE *crosses to the hall door and exits.* I'd really hate that. *Calling.* Don't stand at the door talking. If there is a caller bring them right in. If it is a mistake send them away. Do you hear me, Lillie? *She sits quietly thinking. There is a mumbled conversation in the hall.* Come in. Lillie, bring them in here. LILLIE *enters hesitantly with* CLOVIS MITCHELL. *He is twenty-six, dressed in poorly fitting clothes, and horribly deformed. He walks with great effort, his right leg being a good four inches shorter than his left and his right arm paralyzed. However, his face is beautiful as that of a slender Boticelli angel.*

LILLIE: This is my sister, Althea Pergande.

ALTHEA: *a gesture of welcome.* Come in young man, come in. *He hands her a card.* Clovis Mitchell, assistant, Church of the Living God . . . You're from the tent revival down the street.

CLOVIS: *a smile angelic.* Yes.

ALTHEA: *Searching his face.* I have been reading about you in the paper.

CLOVIS: *Modestly.* We took a little ad.

ALTHEA: It was on the obituary page. I saw it right away. And a neighbor told my sister Lillie that you were there. CLOVIS *takes a step nearer.*

CLOVIS: We've been there three nights, this is our fourth night.

ALTHEA: Interesting work, is it? Preaching and traveling.

CLOVIS: I don't preach.

ALTHEA: Oh?

CLOVIS: I am not gifted. I just try to lead people to our pastor. He is a great preacher. My job is to bring people to him. I witness, but I don't preach.

ALTHEA: *smiling.* Did you come to lead *us* to him?

CLOVIS: Yes. I want to lead everyone to him.

LILLIE: *crossing down.* A neighbor told me tonight. Mrs. Grim, down the street told me . . .

ALTHEA: Mrs. Grim told my sister that she had been and was young again.

LILLIE: *impulsively.* And she looked it. She smiled, as old as she is, she smiled.

CLOVIS: *humbly.* The preacher does things like that, he makes the old ones young again, he makes the young ones age in mind . . . *Almost a prayer.* He inspires us to find the best of our qualities and make more of them. Might I sit down, walking is not easy yet.

LILLIE: I'm sorry, of course. *Leading him to the chair, center.*

ALTHEA: *I* can understand that. Take the chair. *Indicating the chair center near the daybed.* As you can see I don't walk. I haven't walked in the longest time. I had polio. Sister Lillie there brought it to me as gift for my birthday. *She wheels her chair closer to him.* My infirmity is obvious to the world. So is yours. *We* have a handicap.

CLOVIS: Or a blessing.

ALTHEA: I don't look on it as a blessing. Are you a polio case?

CLOVIS: I was born this way.

ALTHEA: I wasn't. I walked and remember walking. I ran. You don't remember walking, it's not so bad.

CLOVIS: I suppose not. I tire easily, I don't mind. Walking.

ALTHEA: *Looking at his legs.* More like waddling. Duck-like.

LILLIE: *shocked.* Althea.

ALTHEA: Be still, Lillie. *To* CLOVIS. My sister interferes occasionally. I . . . am a truth speaker. At my age there's no reason not to be.

CLOVIS: *laughing* You're right. *To* LILLIE. It's true, I do waddle like a duck. When I was a boy, the other fellows would follow me to school . . . *He makes a quacking noise.* They still call me duck legs Mitchell at home.

LILLIE: Cruel. *She looks at* ALTHEA *with meaning.*

CLOVIS: *lightly.* I didn't mind.

ALTHEA: Of course not. He faces fact. Lillie, if you'd stop trying to hide your shaky old hands, you'd be better off. Just hold them out and let them tremble in the wind. *To* CLOVIS. Don't you think, young man?

CLOVIS: We each have a way of doing things, I don't know mine is better than anyone else's.

ALTHEA: *cozily.* You're too young to be sure of yourself.

CLOVIS: Not really . . .

ALTHEA: How old are you?

LILLIE: My sister doesn't mean to . . .

ALTHEA: *roughly.* I asked him how old he is.

LILLIE: Please, Althea.

CLOVIS: *lightly.* I'm twenty-six.

ALTHEA: You look older. I guess it's the pain.

CLOVIS: I have no pain.

ALTHEA: Then you . . . don't feel for other people?

CLOVIS: No. I can only feel myself. I try . . . I can try to understand how other people might feel. But I can't. *He rises.*

LILLIE: *crossing to him.* Don't get up.

ALTHEA: *her facade of bitterness completely gone.* No, stay a while and rest.

CLOVIS: *smiling.* I can't. I want to reach so many people. We had only twelve last night. In a tent that holds a thousand, there were twelve people. I had walked all day, I talked to hundreds. Fifty people said they'd come, but only twelve came and some of those I didn't even see before. I don't have much time left. It'll be time to start soon.

LILLIE: *impulsively.* I want to come.

ALTHEA: *to* LILLIE. Don't be ridiculous, your head jumping back and forth would disturb everyone there. You don't go out anymore . . . *To* CLOVIS. And of course, I don't go out anymore. *Wheeling herself toward the window.* You see, I can't even get into the window. I don't see the sun. I don't see people. *Turning around.* This is my universe. For sixty years almost.

LILLIE: I want to go.

ALTHEA: Nonsense. You'll stay here. *To* CLOVIS. My sister is foolish enough to think she would be made young, the palsy gone, if she could get there. *To* LILLIE. How would you get there, you don't know your way around the world anymore?

CLOVIS: *smiling.* I would take her.

ALTHEA: *laughing, her head thrown back.* The lame leading the lamer. What a pair you two would make. *Wheels downstage center.*

LILLIE: My sister can be unkind.

CLOVIS: *crossing to the door.* I'll come back at a quarter of eight. I'll take you. *Kindly, to* ALTHEA. You'll see, it'll be all right. *Turning back.* Why can't you go? I'll push you.

ALTHEA: *moved.* No, I'm afraid I couldn't go . . .

LILLIE: *crossing to her and kneeling slightly.* Please, Althea, let's try. You say so often, what do we have to lose, whatever's waiting can happen now. Couldn't we try?

ALTHEA: No. There is no place for me out there. Or you either for that matter.

LILLIE: Please, couldn't we . . .

ALTHEA: *undecided.* Give me a while to think it out. *To* CLOVIS. How long will you be here?

CLOVIS: Tonight's our last night. *Apologetically.* I wish I could have found you before. But it's not too late. It's not too late.

LILLIE: *pleading.* No, Althea. It's not too late.

ALTHEA: *sharply.* I said I'd study it. I will. I didn't say no.

LILLIE: But you will. You always say no.

ALTHEA: I do not. I do not always say no.

LILLIE: *defeated almost.* You will, I know you will.

CLOVIS: *to* LILLIE. Give her a time to think. I'll be back. *He starts to go.*

ALTHEA: *suddenly.* Wait!

CLOVIS: *turning.* Yes?

ALTHEA: Stay a moment.

CLOVIS: *with hesitation.* I have so many people to see.

ALTHEA: Then we're not important.*She turns her back to him.*

CLOVIS: *quietly.* Everyone's important.

ALTHEA: But we're not. *Turning back to him.* But we don't feel we are. No, go on. Find your crowds. We've managed so long, a little longer won't bother. It's really all right. *She smiles.*

CLOVIS: I can stay a little while.

LILLIE: *quickly.* And have some coffee.

CLOVIS: *smiling at her.* I'd like some coffee. I don't want to . . .

LILLIE: It's easy. I'll hurry. *She walks toward the dining room.*

ALTHEA: Yes, hurry. Don't stand there shaking, hurry and fix the coffee. LILLIE *quickly exits to the kitchen.* You see my sister is a person of no direction. She has required guidance. She has been intelligent, but she has needed to be told when and where to move. *Looking at her legs.* If I had not been crippled . . . I would be here in all probability anyway, caring for her. I think perhaps that's what I have resented most . . . the knowledge that if I could have spent my life walking straight as an arrow, nothing really would have been changed. Do you know what I mean?

CLOVIS: I don't know. I don't understand a lot.

ALTHEA: *with sweetness.* It takes growing old.

CLOVIS: I don't know that I will understand then.

ALTHEA: *smiling.* You'll have to find it out for yourself. The right time. Tell me, do you believe in your preacher?

CLOVIS: I believe he speaks with the voice of God.

ALTHEA: But you said that you can only feel for yourself.

CLOVIS: That is true, but I can hear with understanding and take the faith the way I hear it. Do you have faith?

ALTHEA: *laughing scornfully.* The faith! I have faith in my ability to control my world . . . here. Perhaps that's why I don't go out.

CLOVIS: Let me tell you a story. My arm . . . *He takes his right arm and shakes it with his left hand. . . .* is heavy, sometimes more than others. Today it was very heavy. I have walked the streets for three days. I woke this morning. My arm was like a lead pipe. I said I can't go today. I can't go out and drag this arm with me. And as I said this to myself, I heard the voice of God. *Striking a pose.* The cross was heavy on the Via Dolorosa. So I pulled on my clothes and I walked the streets.

ALTHEA: How ostentatious of you to hear that.

CLOVIS: Yes, perhaps it was.

ALTHEA: A rationalization.

CLOVIS: Perhaps.

ALTHEA: Why do you believe in him? The preacher.

CLOVIS: Because he is kind.

ALTHEA: Because he is kind?

CLOVIS: Yes.

ALTHEA: Nothing else?

CLOVIS: When he leaves people they are kinder to each other.

ALTHEA: There are kind people everywhere.

CLOVIS: I don't deny it.

ALTHEA: Then why him. You follow and drag your arm along. For what? I'll tell you what. Your own self-aggrandizement. You want to see in eyes . . . what a wonderful man is . . . What's your name?

CLOVIS: Clovis . . . Clovis Mitchell. I hadn't thought about it like that. Perhaps I do. But if I can contribute even that way, does it matter so much? Does the motivation for goodness require goodness?

ALTHEA: For it to be real it does. Let me tell you a story about me. I was going to be an actress. I memorized Roxanne, Celia, Juliet. I learned them all and I never got to use them. I was twisted in a wringing motion and left like this. And all the words were wasted. Useless. *Lightly.* So I became a poet, a poetess. And no one ever read any of my poems, because none of them were ever published. So I told them to my sister, who has such fierce needs. *Turning from him slightly.* It is not enough to hold the poems in your head.

CLOVIS: *excitedly.* Exactly. It is not enough to touch kindness and not share it.

ALTHEA: Something one creates is different from an ideal.

CLOVIS: This is no difference.

ALTHEA: I don't care for theology.

CLOVIS: *quietly.* I care for everything.

ALTHEA: Honestly?

CLOVIS: I think so.

ALTHEA: Before my sister brings the coffee. I have not been kind to her . . . because she did not want kindness.

CLOVIS: *earnestly.* Everyone wants kindness.

ALTHEA: *shaking her head.* Not everyone. Some want to be controlled, to be kicked in one way or another. That's the way Lillie is.

CLOVIS: It this your rationalization?

ALTHEA: *smiling*. We reverse our roles.

CLOVIS: Often.

ALTHEA: An exercise. Human contact is an exercise.

CLOVIS: *suddenly*. Please come tonight. I think you may learn something. Something of value.

ALTHEA: I don't know. I have too much to lose, too little to gain.

CLOVIS: *softly*. What do you have to lose?

ALTHEA: You couldn't understand.

CLOVIS: I would try.

ALTHEA: *coming closer to him*. All right. Let me explain my sister. She has been a very passive gentle thing . . . all her life. As a child she cried when leaves fell from the trees, when flowers died.

CLOVIS: I can see her gentleness.

ALTHEA: And she could do nothing to prevent dying and aging . . . We had funerals for flowers. There is a cemetery for marigolds in the back yard. CLOVIS *does not comprehend*. You see you cannot understand. *She turns from him somewhat*. Because I still do not really understand either. Somehow she fixed on guilt and it's expiation. *Turning back to him*. There, I'm being much too serious.

CLOVIS: No . . . you have needed someone.

ALTHEA: Yes, someone to talk to. I forget my role. It is very difficult for me to be myself. *Laughing softly*. I don't always remember who I am.

CLOVIS: You could sit in the front row.

ALTHEA: Your preacher could help me be myself?

CLOVIS: *eagerly*. Yes, he can do that too.

ALTHEA: With twelve out of fifty who come. You are a parable.

CLOVIS: No. I don't mean to be.

ALTHEA: Your preacher is not God?

CLOVIS: Oh no. He speaks well. He helps people to help each other. That's all. I never meant . . .

ALTHEA: *laughing*. It's all right. When you are young, you can be so very earnest. I tease. I've had to. *Seriously*. You have brought something with you tonight. Do you know what it is?

CLOVIS: What?

ALTHEA: A faint, far, feel of hope. *Pleased with herself*. That's an alliteration.

CLOVIS: I don't know what that means.

ALTHEA: Nothing. Just a figure of speech. *In a very cross voice*. Lillie, hurry up in the kitchen. I don't know why you take so long to do everything. *Louder*. Don't forget about the newspaper. *To* CLOVIS. The concept of kidness can be . . . the opposite. Don't you think?

CLOVIS: I don't know. *He is growing impatient to leave*.

ALTHEA: *aware*. You wish to leave, don't you? There is such fatigability in doing good.

CLOVIS: *shaking his head.* No. I want people to hear him tonight. More than a dozen. There are other streets and almost no time at all.

ALTHEA: *calling.* Lillie!

LILLIE: *off-stage.* I am.

ALTHEA: *to* CLOVIS. She'll be here in a minute. You will have your coffee and you shall go. On your way back, stop here and I'll let you know if we can go.

CLOVIS: You will be happy if you go. I promise that.

ALTHEA: *musing.* Can happiness happen so easily?

CLOVIS: It has, it has. I've seen it.

ALTHEA: Then I should like to see it. Young man, I am an old cynic, I am an old cynic, I am not unwise. You have no idea how much I have learned . . . *A soft laugh.* . . . from the obituary page. LILLIE *enters with a tray, three cups of coffee.*

LILLIE: *to* CLOVIS. I did not know how you liked it.

CLOVIS: Anyway . . . black.

LILLIE: I thought you might. *To* ALTHEA. I tried to do yours just like you want it, if you want coffee.

ALTHEA: Indeed I do. LILLIE *gives them each a cup.* Smells very nice. *She tastes it.* Lillie it's wonderful. I never tasted coffee so good.

LILLIE: *incredulous.* I . . . I . . . I . . .

CLOVIS: It is good. You make a fine cup of coffee, Miss Pergande. And I think your sister is planning to come and hear the pastor.

LILLIE: Oh, Althea, could we?

ALTHEA: Perhaps. I think we might. With the help of this young man I think we might.

LILLIE: *taking her cup to the window, she sits.* Do we have the right clothes?

CLOVIS: It doesn't matter what you wear. You're both fine just as you are.

LILLIE: This? *Indicating her dress, ashamed.*

CLOVIS: Is fine. ALTHEA *is thinking.* The Lord looks with favor on the meek and poor.

ALTHEA: That's ostentation.

CLOVIS: I'm quoting. I do not speak for God.

LILLIE: When is the meeting?

CLOVIS: In about an hour. I'm trying to fill the first aisle anyway. It is the last night. Tomorrow we'll be somewhere else.

ALTHEA: Where?

CLOVIS: I don't know. It doesn't matter. *Standing.* Thank you for the coffee. Miss Lillie, it was the very best coffee I ever had. Miss Althea, you make me think. I've got to rearrange my mind a little.

LILLIE: *rising.* Thank you for coming. We've held you long enough.

ALTHEA: Yes, we have. Thank you for coming. *Suddenly.* We *will* go. Lillie, what have we got to lose? We *will* go. With a little pride. Young man, is it all right to go with a little pride.

CLOVIS: I think in whatever guise you go you gain something. Well, you see for yourself. *Crossing to the door.* I want to give you something . . . *He puts his cup on the library table.* I want to say a prayer here with you.

ALTHEA: *quickly.* I thought you said you didn't preach.

CLOVIS: I don't. But I do pray.

ALTHEA: I don't think we're ready for prayers yet. Lillie, do you? What do you want? LILLIE *crosses to the door.*

LILLIE: *a new tone for her, a stronger voice.* No, not now. I . . . don't think we're ready for prayers.

CLOVIS: All right. Then I want to give you my book. *He takes a pocket book version of the New Testament from his pocket.* It's all we can give. *Sadly.* We don't have money. I'll be back in a little while. I'll be proud to take you . . . you'll be bright stars, the brightest there. *A building exultation.* And after the service, I'll bring you back here and Miss Lillie, you can fix more coffee and we can talk of dreams. We can talk of dreams. *He quickly exits into the hall.* LILLIE *follows, the door is heard closing and she rapidly reappears. She is flushed, a high state of excitement.*

LILLIE: *breathlessly.* Are we really going, Althea?

ALTHEA: If you want to.

LILLIE: I want to go if you want to go. I never thought *you'd* want to go.

ALTHEA: *lightly.* I never thought I would dare. Our young man Clovis has touched a chord someplace. *Jocular.* If nothing more than to see Mrs. Grim made young.

LILLIE: And us. Maybe we'll smile.

ALTHEA: *smiling.* I'm smiling now. See. And maybe in the Spring, we can hire a boy to take us to the park. We'll see leaves and blossoms . . . and . . . *Trailing off.*

LILLIE: *flatly.* There'll be many people in the park.

ALTHEA: I think maybe we can look at them.

LILLIE: *frightened.* The children didn't worry me. Not very much. It was . . . the . . . parents.

ALTHEA: *crossing to the table and picking up the Bible.* It's a Bible. He left us his Bible.

LILLIE: *crossing to the window.* It's very dark outside.

ALTHEA: I know, it's night.

LILLIE: There are people in the dark as well as in the park.

ALTHEA: *brightly.* I want to see Mrs. Grim smile. You did and I want to.

LILLIE: Mrs. Grim smiled.

ALTHEA: That's why we're going. LILLIE *crosses to her.*

LILLIE: Was the coffee really all right?

ALTHEA: Yes, dear. It was fine.

LILLIE: You never said it was fine before. You said it wasn't fit to drink.

ALTHEA: I was wrong.

LILLIE: I made it the same way I always do. First I boiled the water and scalded the pot and the . . .

ALTHEA: It was wonderful. I was wrong before. Lillie, I think perhaps it's time for a change.

LILLIE: *unhearing.* Then I put the coffee in . . .

ALTHEA: It was very good.

LILLIE: And the eggshell. That's for clarification. You always wanted everything to be so clear. *Coming close to her.*

ALTHEA: *trying to get this across.* I said I might have been wrong. The way I did things might have been wrong.

LILLIE: Oh no. You weren't wrong. I didn't try hard enough to please you. I've always felt so guilty.

ALTHEA: It is time for guilt to go. A new basis.

LILLIE: There isn't time. There never was.

ALTHEA: I gave up too easily. I was afraid to try . . . afraid of failure.

LILLIE: In the dark . . .

ALTHEA: *quick.* We may find light. It's worth a chance. Lillie, is it worth a chance? It's too late to have anything to lose. Isn't it?

LILLIE: *fearful.* In the dark are people. Suppose we are attacked.

ALTHEA: People don't attack people.

LILLIE: They do. You said they do. We can't ever go outside again because we'll be attacked, you said it. I remember you said it.

ALTHEA: I was wrong.

LILLIE: What's wrong and right? How can I tell what's wrong and right?

ALTHEA: *gently.* I'll always tell you. I'll tell you, Lillie. You don't have to worry about it.

LILLIE: *becoming more and more agitated and pacing about the room.* I don't want to go.

ALTHEA: Yes, Lillie, you wanted to go.

LILLIE: *childishly.* I don't now. I don't want to go now. I thought I did, but now I know I don't.

ALTHEA: *pleading.* Dearest, try, let's try.

LILLIE: No.

ALTHEA: Just once, let's try.

LILLIE: *near hysteria.* You can't abdicate the responsibility.

ALTHEA: *gently.* I'm not. Lillie, sit down . . . for a moment. Let me explain it to you.

LILLIE: I am not a child to be explained to.

ALTHEA: I know you're not a child.

LILLIE: Then why do you treat me like one.

ALTHEA: Oh Lillie. I am treating you like my sister.

LILLIE: I was guilty. It was all my fault. All the sins, all the pains . . .

ALTHEA: *still very gentle*. They've been gone so long.

LILLIE: Not long enough. *Looking about*. They're not gone. They're here. Here where I want them to be. Look around you.

ALTHEA: *tired*. I don't have to look.

LILLIE: I'm not going. I don't care what you say. I'm not going.

ALTHEA: *soothing*. All right. We won't go. Not this time.

LILLIE: *even more fearful*. What do you mean, not this time?

ALTHEA: Just what I said. There may be another time. You may feel better another time.

LILLIE: I won't feel better if I have to think there is going to be a time. You don't understand at all.

ALTHEA: I understand too well. *Wearily*. Isn't there any other way?

LILLIE: *quieter*. No. We were happy once.

ALTHEA: We were young once, too. *Sadly*. I think we have both expected too much.

LILLIE: *coldly*. You would throw it out the door, all the balance.

ALTHEA: Lillie, I am tired and I am very old. And I would like to spend a peaceful day.

LILLIE: *shouting*. You don't care about me. You never cared about me. You used and used us all. The only thing you cared about was domination. DOMINATION.

ALTHEA: *thinking aloud*. He'll be back.

LILLIE: Who? Who?

ALTHEA: The young man. Clovis.

LILLIE: *taking the Bible from* ALTHEA, *she crosses to the door. The front door is heard opening and closing, the bolts being drawn.* Now. ALTHEA *is crying softly.* I threw the Bible in the mud. He can't help but step on it. And I bolted the door and he can't ever get back in here again. Not ever. *She crosses to the windows and pulls the drapes tightly without looking out.* And they can't see in. And I don't care about your paper. Do you hear? I don't care about your paper anymore. *She stands in the center of the window and taking the scissors from the chair, she begins to slash at her needlepoint.*

ALTHEA: *still crying.* Stop it. Stop. *Rapidly, her voice quavering.* Sister Lillie bent and shaking, head awobble, knees shaking, killed her sister and her brother, killed her father and her mother. LILLIE, *dazed, puts down the shears.* Saying it was inadvertent. Saying that she didn't meant it.

LILLIE: *softly smiling.* I am going to cover my ears, Althea.

ALTHEA: *rough.* You wouldn't.

LILLIE: I will, I will.

ALTHEA: Saying it was accidental. LILLIE *covers her ears, her face transfigured.* That the poison and the pistol and the other means of murder. LILLIE *slowly crosses to the day bed and lies down, her hands still covering her ears.* Were acts of God, coincidental. *Turning away.* Lillie never harmed a flower.

LILLIE: *far away.* I can't hear you.

ALTHEA: Let us make an illusion, you and I. *The doorbell rings.* That we have sometime loved each other. *She crosses to the bed and covers* LILLIE *with a quilt.* Because of gentleness. *The doorbell rings again.* Knowing too much and knowing too little. Sleep a while, you are right. It is too late to change anything. ALTHEA *wheels her chair center and sits, her face hardened.*

CURTAIN

The Telegram

BY FRAN LOHMAN

THE TELEGRAM was originally presented by Virginia Aquino and Harry Orzello at WPA, 333 Bowery, New York City, in April, 1971. The production was directed by Barbara Rosoff and featured the following actors:

MRS. . . . . Enid Edelman
MR. . . . . Tony Johnson

Approximate playing time: 10 minutes

TV noises.

MRS.: It's very cloudy out. How come it's cloudy when the weather man said fair?

MR.: Sssh. Bases loaded. Let's get this guy out. STRIKE! Attaboy!

MRS.: The humidity is very high. I can feel it in my feet.

MR.: Called strike. The side is retired. Last half of the ninth coming up.

MRS.: Where's the telegram?

MR.: Right here. In my pocket.

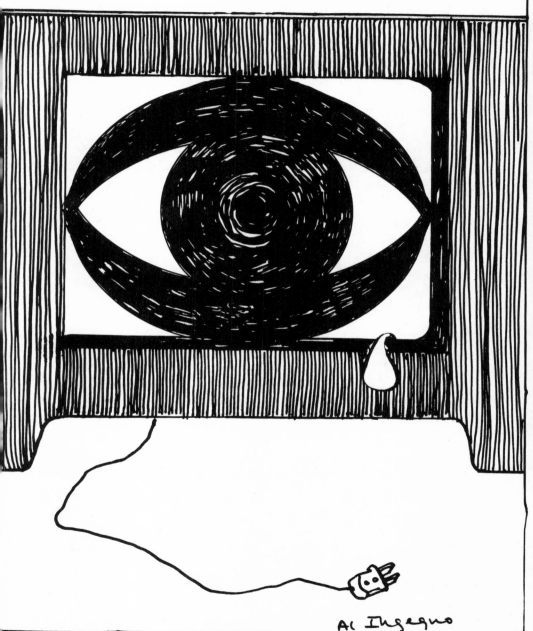

Al Ingegno

MRS.: I want to see it.

MR.: What a ball game!

MRS.: Why do you wrinkle it up that way?

MR.: Like the man says, time out for a beer.

MRS.: You know, we ought to do something. Make a complaint or something. We always talk about doing something, but we never do. Maybe we should go to Washington.

MR.: *drinking the beer.* All American bottom of the ninth . . . down the hatch!

MRS.: We could lie down . . . in the road . . . I've seen them do it on TV.

MR.: Last chance you guys, come on let's get some runs!

MRS.: "HAS been reported missing . . ." "has BEEN reported missing . . ." "has been REPORTED missing . . ." "has been reported MISSING . . ." Which way do you think it sounds better?

MR.: Hooo Haaa . . . a base hit! Come on now, knock him in!

MRS.: I know. We could call somebody up. The President. We could call him up tonight and ask him . . . Except . . . the Academy Awards are on tonight.

MR.: What a pitch! What are you waiting for you bum!

MRS.: What an academy award pitch missing in action.

MR.: Hey . . . there's a long one. Not long enough. Good catch!

MRS.: "We regret to inform you . . ." I regret, you regret, he regrets, we regret . . .

MR.: Looks like a hit . . . no . . . he's got it . . . double play!

MRS. It's hard to remember his face now . . .

MR.: Well . . . that's the series. Another season over. Three pennant races since we got the telegram. Let me have it.

MRS.: Don't grab it like that.

MR.: Why do you hold it so tight?

MRS.: My favorite commercial. Look at that. Gets all the dirt out. She's pretty. A good little homemaker.

MR.: We need a new one of these . . . this one's getting all worn out.

MRS.: *singing and dancing.* Wash day rock
                          Wash day roll
                          Wash day rock and roll.

MR.: We should have had another one. A girl maybe . . .

MRS.: It's true. Some stains just don't come out.

MR.: Missing doesn't mean dead.

MRS.: He's right. Even hard scrubbing and bleaching doesn't take them out.

MR.: It's too late now. Nothing anyone can do.

MRS.: Give me the telegram.

MR.: He didn't want to go. *Handing it to her.*

MRS.: It's clearing up. Maybe the sun will come out after all. *Taking it.* We used to take walks when the weather was nice.

MR.: There's a car for you . . . built like a rocket ship.

MRS.: *putting the telegram in her dress.* Don't go away . . .

MR.: It's time to play . . .

MRS.: Your lucky day . . .

MR.: The world's most popular

MRS.: Name of the game . . .

MR.: Always the same.

MRS.: Ohh . . . aren't they sweet.

MR.: Let's welcome our first couple . . .

MRS.: I wonder why they have to be married . . .

MR.: There's the prize. A complete bedroom set.

MRS.: Everything matching.

MR.: Get a banana . . . quick.

MRS.: In the bowl . . . in the bowl.

MR.: Here . . .

MRS.: Hurry up . . . put it under my chin.

MR.: Don't get excited . . . it never works out when you get excited . . .

MRS.: We've never done it with a banana before. You're not supposed to use your hands . . . you've got to follow the rules . . .

MR.: Your head's in the way.

MRS.: Quick . . . start peeling it . . . hurry up . . . no . . . not with your hands . . . use your teeth. Ouch . . . you're standing on my feet . . . Oooh . . . there's the bell . . . we didn't even get started.

MR.: The other couple is wearing sneakers, that's why. See?

MRS.: Evelyn went down to the show. She says it's all rehearsed anyway.

MR.: Look. There's the bedroom set.

MRS.: We never get anything new. Our bed is a mess. It's all lumpy. And it makes noise all night. I hear you getting in and out of bed all night.

MR.: I can't sleep any more . . . asleep . . . it all seems the same. Where's the telegram?

MRS.: Here. Now they have to keep the rubber ball in the air. Where's our rubber ball?

MR.: Look out . . . let go. Now you tore it. Right in half. Why do you keep it folded up so small?

MRS.: I didn't fold it up . . . it came that way . . . in the envelope.

MR.: You can't even read it.

MRS.: Fold it up. Folderol. Where did you put our rubber ball.

MR.: This one's no good any more. Maybe we could get a new one.

MR.: Can't even see the words any more. In two pieces.

MRS.: Give it to me.

MRS.: Don't keep it in your dress.

MRS.: Where then . . . where?

MR.: A trip to Jamaica . . . The ball, the ball, the ball, get the ball.

MR.: We're missing out on the trip to Jamaica.

MRS.: We should burn it . . . yes . . . that's what we should do.

MR.: Five seconds, 4, 3.

MRS.: Here, hold the pieces.

MR.: Look out . . . I can't see . . . 3, 2.

MRS.: *lighting a match.* Don't wiggle them.

MR.: Oooh. Pretty.

MRS.: *lighting one piece of the telegram.* There.

MR.: Now this one. Ouch it's hot. *Dropping the pieces. Organ music from the TV. They observe the burnt pieces.*

MR.: Crispy . . .

MRS.: Sealed in . . .

MR.: Easy spreading . . .

BOTH: Super proven

      Extra soothing
      Soft and fluffy
      Puffy wuffy

MRS.: Baby gentle

MR.: Tender wender. *Curling up on floor.*

MRS.: Feels like poo poo

MR.: Buy me doo doo

MRS. Gimmee goo goo

BOTH: Da da. Ma ma. Can or ba ba.
      Botty botty
      doody doody

BOTH: Ma
      Ba
       Da
        Wa
         Waaah waah

They curl up in front of the TV. *Organ music plays Rock a Bye Baby.*

CURTAIN

The Heist

BY ROBERT REINHOLD

THE HEIST was originally presented by Viktor Allen at the Omni Theater Club, 145 West 18th Street, New York City, in January, 1971. The production was directed by Viktor Allen and featured the following actors:

WAFER	Eugene A. Draper
YOUNG WAFER	Mierre
WAFER II	Dennis Southers
MRS. NACH	Linda Robbins
MRS. BARR	Cassandra Danz
COP	Garry Mitchel

Approximate playing time: 35 minutes

The livingroom of an apartment in a modern city. Evening. WAFER, *a squarely-built middle-aged man, is seated in armchair, very rigidly, watching television.* YOUNG WAFER, *a husky man in his twenties, seems to be in the process of redecorating room. He moves objects of furniture around, although he has a tendency to place them near the front door, upstage right. There is a window stage left.*

WAFER: Have you seen the newspapers?

YOUNG WAFER: I saw the newspaper on the floor.

WAFER: Why didn't you pick it up?

YOUNG WAFER: I thought you'd read it.

WAFER: Where is the newspaper?

YOUNG WAFER: I moved the armchair over it.

WAFER: Get it.

YOUNG WAFER: You sound just like a father.

WAFER: . . . well?

YOUNG WAFER: I'll work around here but I won't kiss your ass.

WAFER: Too bad.

YOUNG WAFER: Look, Wafer, if you want the newspaper you get it yourself.

WAFER: I told you to call me father the way you should.

YOUNG WAFER: I will when you rate being called father.

WAFER: You're on record as Young Wafer.

YOUNG WAFER: When I was born I wasn't listed as Young Wafer in the newspapers.

WAFER: Get me the newspaper.

YOUNG WAFER: Get your own newspaper.

WAFER: I'm tired.

YOUNG WAFER: You're a lazy bastard.

WAFER: Go on arranging the furniture.

YOUNG WAFER: I hope we got time.

WAFER: Certainly we've got time.

YOUNG WAFER: I like to get things done on time.

WAFER: Before you go on to the next job.

YOUNG WAFER: Why shouldn't I be prepared?

WAFER: You're too conscientious.

YOUNG WAFER: One of us has to be conscientious.

WAFER: Let it be the son.

YOUNG WAFER: It's always the son.

WAFER: I'm tired of this program.

YOUNG WAFER: Why don't you turn it off then?

WAFER: It requires too much effort.

YOUNG WAFER: *Pulling out plug of* TV *set, then pushing set away from him and moving it near door, screen toward wall.* Now you won't have problems.

WAFER: What do you want me to do while you arrange the furniture?

YOUNG WAFER: Listen for someone coming if you want to.

WAFER: I don't think we're expecting any visitors.

YOUNG WAFER: We've always got visitors.

WAFER: Not if we're careful.

YOUNG WAFER: I can't avoid them.

WAFER: *Getting up, pacing floor.* Boy, kid, I'm upset.

YOUNG WAFER: What the hell do you have to be upset about?

WAFER: We always have to be afraid of visitors.

YOUNG WAFER: *Going to him, touching his shoulder.* Don't think about them.

WAFER: I like privacy.

YOUNG WAFER: So do I.

WAFER: Domestic scene.

YOUNG WAFER: I dig it.

WAFER: Well, then, why can't I . . . we . . .?

YOUNG WAFER: Some day we'll afford it.

WAFER: A place for ourselves without visitors.

YOUNG WAFER: *Going back to moving furniture.* But right now we got to prepare.

WAFER: *Grumbling.* Removing furniture this time of night.

YOUNG WAFER: What the hell, this apartment's going to be refurnished.

WAFER: And what an expense!

YOUNG WAFER: Why should we worry?

WAFER: It's our worry.

YOUNG WAFER: Not in the long run.

WAFER: I'm very sensitive.

YOUNG WAFER: Well get your sensitive fingers on this sideboard and push. *Reluctantly* WAFER *helps him move large sideboard toward front door.*

WAFER: *Listening suddenly.* What was the noise?

YOUNG WAFER: It could be the . . . moving men.

WAFER: Why are they coming so late?

YOUNG WAFER: It's always better that way.

WAFER: I can hear two pair of feet way down on the staircase.

YOUNG WAFER: This apartment house has a very creaky staircase.

WAFER: *Still listening, whispering.* How many moving men are we expecting?

YOUNG WAFER: Also whispering. Seven.

WAFER: You arranged for seven with the . . . people?

YOUNG WAFER: A very reliable . . . company.

WAFER: Well then if it's only seven coming up we've got visitors and you know how I feel about visitors.

YOUNG WAFER: How do you know the feet on the goddamned staircase belong to visitors?

WAFER: I just feel it in the feet.

YOUNG WAFER: Well if those are visitors, those are visitors who weren't expected. *Feet are heard coming closer and closer. They stop outside door. A key is heard in the lock.*

WAFER: The lights! YOUNG WAFER *switches off lights suddenly.* WAFER *and* YOUNG WAFER *hide behind furniture. Silence. Door opens and two people come into livingroom. Door closes.*

VOICE OF MAN: *Resembling* WAFER'S. What is the . . .?

VOICE OF SECOND MAN: *Resembling* YOUNG WAFER'S. Something's gone wrong in here.

VOICE OF MAN: A sideboard is right by the . . .

VOICE OF SECOND MAN: And a cocktail table is rubbing my . . .

VOICE OF MAN: It's not as we . . .

VOICE OF SECOND MAN: Someone has beaten us to it.

VOICE OF MAN: Turn on the lights.

VOICE OF SECOND MAN: *As he turns, takes out flashlight, switches it on, and prowls through darkness.* They got the television by the light-switch.

VOICE OF MAN: Put the lights on quick!

VOICE OF SECOND MAN: Give me a minute, you bastard. *He switches on light.* MAN *and* SECOND MAN *are seen in overcoats, staring. They uncannily resemle* WAFER *and* YOUNG WAFER. *They remove overcoats rapidly, still looking around.*

MAN: Have you seen the newspaper?

SECOND MAN: I saw it on the floor when we were sitting here before, but why do you want it?

MAN: Information, you idiot, and why didn't you pick it up?

SECOND MAN: I thought you read it.

MAN: Where's the newspaper now?

SECOND MAN: *Seeing it under armchair.* A chair was moved over it. *He gets the newspaper, brings it to* MAN.

MAN: *Rifling through newspaper.* Now there must be some mention of . . .

SECOND MAN: What are you looking for?

MAN: Burglaries, burglaries, news of some . . .

SECOND MAN: Does it say anything?

MAN: *Reading something that horrifies him.* It says too much. *He angrily throws newspaper across room where it hits the floor by the window.*

SECOND MAN: The condition of this place makes me sick.

MAN: Me also.

SECOND MAN: *Suddenly seeing* YOUNG WAFER *crouching behind sideboard.* You . . .

MAN: *Discovering* WAFER *behind the* TV *set.* You . . . MAN *and* SECOND MAN *lift* WAFER *and* YOUNG WAFER *from crouching positions and push them toward center of room.*

MAN: Now what's your name please?

YOUNG WAFER: Don't *you* ask me that.

SECOND MAN: He must have a name.

WAFER: I'll ask for names.

YOUNG WAFER: We've got the right.

WAFER: It's our apartment.

SECOND MAN: *Your* apartment?

YOUNG WAFER: I got the lease with the signature.

SECOND MAN: You have a lease?

MAN: It's our apartment.

YOUNG WAFER: I'll be damned if it's yours.

MAN: What's the name of the landlord?

WAFER: I never asked and I'm sure you don't know either.

MAN: And what's your name?

WAFER: Wafer.

MAN: Who told you that name?

WAFER: Had it since birth.

YOUNG WAFER: Not quite since birth.

SECOND MAN: Who gave you our name?

MAN: Part of a plot.

WAFER: What plot?

YOUNG WAFER: What?

MAN: *My* name is Wafer.

WAFER: I didn't think anybody else could be named Wafer.

SECOND MAN: Well, I'm also named Wafer . . . his son.

YOUNG WAFER: You do look familiar.

WAFER II: *Staring at* WAFER. A resemblance.

YOUNG WAFER: *Staring at* YOUNG WAFER. A coincidence.

WAFER: What do you want with my place?

WAFER II: What do you want with *mine?*

WAFER: I'm sitting watching television with my son and you come in.

WAFER II: Watching television with the screen to the wall?

WAFER: We were fixing the furniture.

WAFER: You were robbing the furniture.

YOUNG WAFER: We were getting ready to replace the furniture.

WAFER II: You were getting ready to haul if off.

YOUNG WAFER: We were getting ready to send it off to a warehouse in place of new furniture.

WAFER II: Replacing this furniture?

YOUNG WAFER II: Our furniture?

WAFER II: Expensive furniture like this?

WAFER: How do you know it's expensive?

WAFER II: Genuine chippendale, except the television set.

WAFER: That's certainly what it is, along with some original Second Empire.

WAFER II: How do you know it's Second Empire?

WAFER: Because it's *my* furniture.

WAFER II: Which you were trying to throw out?

WAFER: *Rapidly.* Well if you have to know we thought the furniture was too valuable and there's been a lot of burglaries lately, so we thought it'd be safer in storage.

YOUNG WAFER: *Rapidly.* And we were working here getting ready to have the moving men come and put the furniture in the warehouse and bring us some old furniture that looked exactly like it so if any burglars like you bastards'd be coming to haul it off they'd be taking a beating.

WAFER II: You're explaining too much.

YOUNG WAFER II: I don't believe any of that crap.

WAFER: It's the truth.

YOUNG WAFER: I don't know why I got to waste so much time telling you guys the truth.

YOUNG WAFER II: Could you explain it to the cops?

WAFER II: Let's leave the police out of this.

YOUNG WAFER: Why don't you want to go to the cops?

WAFER: Let's not be so anxious to go to the police.

WAFER: I think we should all sit down and discuss this.

WAFER: Well, everybody sit. *They sit.*

YOUNG WAFER II: I don't think we should discuss anything.

WAFER II: What do you propose to do?

YOUNG WAFER II: Throw them out.

WAFER: No.

YOUNG WAFER: Or hand them over to the cops.

WAFER II: No . . . no . . .

WAFER: This is my apartment and no one's going to arrest me.

WAFER II: But it's not your apartment.

WAFER: I just explained to you about the furniture.

WAFER II: No one sends for new furniture at night.

WAFER: The moving men are too busy during the day.

WAFER: But you two are busy at night.

YOUNG WAFER: Busy with furniture.

WAFER II: With *my* furniture.

WAFER: It's not your furniture if it isn't your apartment.

WAFER II: But I live here.

YOUNG WAFER II: I been living more with the . . . old man for seven years.

WAFER: Is the old man your father?

WAFER II: We go by the same name, don't we?

YOUNG WAFER II: *To Young Wafer.* Is *he* yours?

WAFER: Our family relationship's none of your damn business.

WAFER II: I'm only interested in *your* damn business?

WAFER: Which is what?

WAFER II: Breaking into people's apartments and taking your time taking their furniture.

YOUNG WAFER II: *Getting up.* I need a drink.

WAFER II: Get me a scotch.

YOUNG WAFER: The scotch is next to the kitchen sink and I'll have one too.

WAFER II: *To* YOUNG WAFER II, *indicating* YOUNG WAFER. Don't give *him* any of our drinks.

WAFER: You've got a nerve helping yourself to our drinks. YOUNG WAFER II *sits again without going for drinks.*

WAFER II: God knows what else you helped yourself to.

WAFER: I can touch anything I want.

WAFER II: If it isn't my apartment how'd I get in the front door?

WAFER: You managed to open it.

WAFER II: With *my* key.

WAFER: You made a copy.

WAFER II: From what key?

WAFER: I don't know where you managed to find our keys.

YOUNG WAFER: These creeps are in business to find anything.

WAFER: *To* WAFER II. You can't explain anything about what's going on tonight.

WAFER II: I know something about what's going on tonight.

WAFER: Where did you come from?

WAFER II: *Rapidly.* My Son and I were visiting a furniture auction as a matter of fact because we knew the furniture here was much too valuable and too liable to be robbed by people like you.

YOUNG WAFER: *Rapidly.* And we got ourselves a whole suite of new furniture which is going to replace this and as a matter of fact you finks did us a favor by moving the furniture in the direction of the door because it's going through the door as soon as the new furniture is going to be moved in by the moving . . .

WAFER: *Getting up, furious.* You'll never convince me you're not a couple of . . . fakes!

YOUNG WAFER: *Getting up, trying to calm him.* Hold it, Dad.

WAFER: Burglars!

YOUNG WAFER: They seem to feel . . .

WAFER: I told you I didn't like visitors.

WAFER II: *Also furious but still seated.* I never liked visitors myself and tonight I find they've gone ahead of me into my own apartment.

YOUNG WAFER II: *Calming him but still seated.* Look old man, we've got to be logical.

WAFER II: This doesn't call for logic.

YOUNG WAFER II: It calls for the neighbors.

WAFER: Yes, call in the neighbors.

YOUNG WAFER: We can be spotted by our own neighbors.

WAFER II: If they don't recognize their own neighbors then we're living in the wrong kind of neighborhood.

YOUNG WAFER: *Running to door.* I'll get Mrs. Nach.

YOUNG WAFER II: *Getting up, also running to door.* Mrs. Bahr. *They both go out. Silence for a moment.*

WAFER: *Staring strangely at* WAFER II. Before you came in I had great plans for my son and myself.

WAFER II: *Staring strangely at* WAFER. Before my son turned the key in that lock I had plans . . .

YOUNG WAFER *comes in through door, leading* MRS. NACH, *an elderly woman.*

YOUNG WAFER: *To* MRS. NACH, *indicating* WAFER II. Now tell this character who I am.

MRS. NACH: I was drinking my tea.

YOUNG WAFER: You'll go back to your tea when you tell this guy who I am.

MRS. NACH: *Whimpering.* I was drinking my tea.

WAFER: Son, why did you bother Mrs. Nach so late?

YOUNG WAFER: Because it's almost too late.

MRS. NACH: An old woman drinking her tea.

YOUNG WAFER: Who am I?

MRS. NACH: *Looking closely at his face.* Why you're . . .

YOUNG WAFER II *comes in, leading* MRS. BAHR. *She is also an elderly woman, wearing an apron.*

YOUNG WAFER II: *To her, indicating* WAFER. Now tell him.

MRS. BAHR: What did you want me to tell him?

YOUNG WAFER II: *Angry.* Tell him my name.

MRS. BAHR: Why do you want me to tell him your name?

YOUNG WAFER II: Because he doesn't believe it's my name.

MRS. BAHR: Why are you dragging me into your arguments?

MRS. NACH: Let me drink tea.

MRS. BAHR: I was just getting ready to have a bath.

YOUNG WAFER II: You can take a bath when I'm satisfied.

MRS. BAHR: I don't like arguments before taking a bath.

WAFER II: Let Mrs. Bahr take a bath if it's late.

YOUNG WAFER II: It's late!

MRS. BAHR: All right, then you're . . .

YOUNG WAFER II: Well?

MRS. BAHR: *After a pause.* Mr. Wafer.

YOUNG WAFER II: You mean the *younger* Mr. Wafer.

MRS. BAHR: Well you're not the old Mr. Wafer.

WAFER II: Hmm.

MRS. BAHR: I'm sorry.

WAFER: Woman, you're unbalanced.

MRS. BAHR: Who are you?

WAFER: You know who I am.

WAFER II: Well now, you see?

YOUNG WAFER: She's blind.

MRS. BAHR: I got perfect vision without glasses . . . almost.

YOUNG WAFER: *To* MRS. NACH. How many people do you see?

MRS. NACH: *Looking around room.* I see three people.

YOUNG WAFER II: She's cockeyed.

YOUNG WAFER: Don't you wear glasses?

MRS. NASH: I forgot about my glasses. *Puts them on.*

WAFER: Now how many people do you see?

MRS. NACH: Five.

YOUNG WAFER: Well then she sees five people.

MRS. BAHR: I have to take a bath.

YOUNG WAFER: *To* MRS. NACH. And who am I?

MRS. NACH: Why you're Mr. Wafer naturally.

YOUNG WAFER: The *younger* Mr. Wafer.

YOUNG WAFER II: *To* MRS. NACH, *indicating* WAFER II. Who is this man?

MRS. NACH: How should I know?

MRS. BAHR: *To* MRS. NACH. Are you so blind you don't know Mr. Wafer?

MRS. NACH: Let me drink tea.

MRS. BAHR: With your tea kettle and pots keeping me awake.

MRS. NACH: I need my tea like you need a bath.

MRS. BAHR: *You* need a bath.

MRS. NACH: I get a bath from the water from your bathtub leaking through my ceiling.

MRS. BAHR: I don't need you knocking up with a broom.

MRS. NACH: I knock up because you're walking way into the night.

MRS. BAHR: I'm walking into one room and another room and it's my business.

MRS. NACH: Your walking keeps me awake and it's *my* business.

MRS. BAHR: And your hi-fi bouncing on my floor keeps me awake.

MRS. NACH: I'll take you to court again if you keep walking.

MRS. BAHR: And I'll take you to court again if you keep bouncing.

MRS. NACH: I'll take your bathtub to court.

YOUNG WAFER: *Interrupting.* Mrs. Bahr, *this* is my father. *Indicating* WAFER.

MRS. BAHR: Who are you?

YOUNG WAFER: This is *my* house.

YOUNG WAFER II: He broke into it.

MRS. BAHR: It's not my business.

MRS. NACH: *To* YOUNG WAFER II. Who are you?

YOUNG WAFER II: I'm your neighbor.

WAFER: He's a burglar.

MRS. NACH: I got personal problems. *Moves to go but it is intercepted by* YOUNG WAFER II *who restrains her.*

MRS. BAHR: I'm a lonely widow who frightens easily. *Moves to go but is intercepted by* YOUNG WAFER *who restrains her.*

YOUNG WAFER II: I'll prove these guys have taken our name.

YOUNG WAFER: You can prove nothing.

YOUNG WAFER II: Mrs. Bahr, what's my real name?

MRS. BAHR: Well you told me you didn't prefer it to Wafer but I think it's nice.

YOUNG WAFER II: It also begins with a w.

MRS. BAHR: Begins with a w.

YOUNG WAFER: E-I-S-S

MRS. BAHR: Is that how you spell Weiss? YOUNG WAFER II *smiles jubilantly.*

WAFER: But Weiss is *our* name.

MRS. NACH: Their name is Weiss and it used to be on the letterbox.

YOUNG WAFER II: *To* WAFER. You must have seen it in the old days on the letterbox.

WAFER: We never had it on the letterbox.

WAFER II: You sound like somebody who was always ashamed of your name.

WAFER: *To* MRS. BAHR. Did we ever have it on the letterbox?

MRS. BAHR: Well I don't remember if Mr. Wafer ever had Weiss on the letterbox.

YOUNG WAFER: Of course we never did.

MRS. BAHR: Who are you?

YOUNG WAFER: I know how we'll finally prove it.

YOUNG WAFER II: You'll never finally prove it.

YOUNG WAFER: Mrs. Bahr, what's my father's business?

MRS. BAHR: Well he operates a . . .

YOUNG WAFER: Pawn?

MRS. BAHR: . . . shop.

YOUNG WAFER: *Satisfied, smiling.* Operates a pawnshop.

WAFER II: Of course I operate a pawnshop.

WAFER: I wouldn't be surprise if you received stolen goods in *your* pawnshop.

MRS. NACH: You know, I heard that Mr. Wafer's pawnshop receives stolen goods. *Recognizing the slip, putting her hand over mouth.*

WAFER: Old lady Nach, you talk too much.

YOUNG WAFER: Maybe old lady Nach's thinking of *his* goddamned shop. *Indicating* WAFER II.

WAFER: But old lady Nach doesn't know him.

YOUNG WAFER: *To* MRS. NACH. Old lady Nach, do you know the location of his pawnshop?

MRS. NACH: Sure, Kingsbridge and Fordham.

WAFER II: Of course that's where it is.

WAFER: Then it must be next to my pawnshop.

YOUNG WAFER: There's only one pawnshop at Kingbridge and Fordham.

WAFER: *To* WAFER II: You look to intellectual to own a pawnshop.

WAFER II: I'm a pawnshop owner who attended Fordham.

WAFER: I also went to Fordham.

WAFER II: No, you don't look as if you went to Fordham.

WAFER: Germans go to Fordham.

WAFER II: Of course Germans go to Fordham because I went to Fordham.

WAFER: I majored in philosophy at Fordham.

WAFER II: I majored in philosophy at Fordham but there we called it metaphysics.

MRS. NACH: Let me drink tea. *Loud knocking at door.*

YOUNG WAFER: *Going to door.* Maybe it's another neighbor.

MRS. BAHR: You're waking up the neighbors.

YOUNG WAFER II: *Also going to door, moving ahead of* YOUNG WAFER. We need more neighbors. *They both open door. A* COP *enters.*

YOUNG WAFER: *Excited, not really noticing him.* Are you a neighbor?

YOUNG WAFER II: Don't you know your own neighbors?

COP: I'm a cop.

WAFER: *Frightened*. I haven't done anything that needs a policeman.

WAFER II: *Even more frightened*. I'm entirely on the side of the law and all policeman.

MRS. NACH: Officer, they won't let me go home.

MRS. BAHR: They won't let me take a bath.

COP: I just got a call from a Mr. . . . Wafer that burglars are over. *A pause*.

WAFER: *To* WAFER II. *You* called the police.

WAFER II: *You* called them.

WAFER: Did you see me call them?

WAFER II: Before we came over.

WAFER: Before you came over why would *I*'ve called to say burglars were over?

WAFER II: And why would *I*'ve called to say burglars were over before I came back to find you were . . .

COP: Over with *what?*

YOUNG WAFER: These people were about to . . .

YOUNG WAFER II: These people were almost over with robbing us.

COP: Who lives here?

WAFER *and* WAFER II: This is my residence.

MRS. BAHR: I live next door.

MRS. NACH: I live downstairs.

COP: *Taking out pad.* You two guys mean your residence is this house.

WAFER: No, I mean this *apartment.*

COP: *To* WAFER II. Then your residence is the next apartment.

WAFER II: No, *this* apartment.

COP: Who came over? WAFER *and* WAFER II *point to each other.* I'll run you both in.

YOUNG WAFER: A guy sits in his own house and gets run in.

YOUNG WAFER II: I come into my house and get run in.

COP: The guy who called didn't sound like neither of you four guys, but maybe a little.

WAFER: Maybe somebody else called you.

COP: I said somebody else called me.

WAFER: I mean somebody called you about another apartment that's being robbed.

COP: The guy said it was this apartment and he saw from the window it was being robbed and he was afraid to come in.

WAFER II: I never saw it being robbed through the window.

COP: But you didn't call me.

MRS. BAHR: He lives here.

MRS. NACH: *Pointing to* WAFER. *He* does.

COP: *Smiling.* Then you both live here . . . with the guy who called.

WAFER: I live here with my son.

COP: They guy who called said he had a son.

WAFER: I don't live here with other people.

WAFER II: *Indicating* WAFER. Why would I want to live here with him and somebody I've never seen who saw me through a window?

COP: Then you admit you were seen through a window robbing this place.

WAFER II: I just said I was seen through a window coming back here to surprise two men who were also seen through a window by somebody who . . . doesn't live here.

COP: How do you know the guy who saw you through the window doesn't live here?

WAFER II: Because I live here.

COP: Alone?

WAFER II: With my son.

COP: Maybe your son saw you through the window.

WAFER II: If there were any windows my son was on the same side of them as me, either out looking in or in looking out.

WAFER: *To* COP. *You* said the man who called was a father.

COP: Keep out of this.

WAFER: I can't because it's my apartment. *Phone rings.* WAFER *and* WAFER II *rush to it.* WAFER *gets there first, picks it up.* Wafer residence.

WAFER II: Who's it for?

WAFER: *Handing phone to* COP. For you.

COP: *Taking phone, into it.* Yes?

WAFER: The voice was very familiar.

COP: *Cupping phone, to everyone.* What's the address again?

ALL: 777 Sedgewick Avenue.

MRS. BAHR: Bronx.

COP: *Into phone.* 777 Sedgewick Avenue . . . Bronx. *He puts it down slowly.*

WAFER: Was it the station house?

COP: It was Mr. Wafer who said he wanted to make sure if he wasn't mistaken and this was really his address, which it is.

WAFER: What Wafer besides myself and this other gentleman here calls himself Wafer?

COP: He said his real name is Weiss.

WAFER II: Of course Wafer is Weiss.

COP: He said he's with his son and he's calling from a street phone-booth across the street and he can see the window and he's afraid to come up.

WAFER: Well, then whoever is calling is calling himself Wafer and Weiss and says he can see us through the window.

COP: But he can see only burglars through the window.

WAFER II: It must be another apartment.

COP: He said it was this apartment.

WAFER: But he didn't see *you* through the window.

COP: He said he coldn't see me through the window but when he heard me on the phone he knew I'd probably surprised the burglars.

WAFER II: Would a burglar pick up the phone and hand it to you?

COP: He would if I were covering him with a pistol.

WAFER: But you weren't covering us with a pistol.

COP: I'm tough and burglars are afraid of tough cops.

YOUNG WAFER: I'm tough too.

YOUNG WAFER II: Me too.

WAFER II: *To* YOUNG WAFER II. Son, are you afraid of him? *A pause.*

YOUNG WAFER II: You know I'm afraid of cops.

YOUNG WAFER: I'm afraid of cops.

COP: Well? *Phone rings again. This time* COP *angrily goes to answer it. He speaks very rapidly into it.* All right you come on up here and we'll see who is what and don't you say that you are what you're not or so help me holy hell I'll drag the truth out of this here damn dump with my PISTOL. *He slams down phone.*

MRS. BHARS *Frightened.* Did I hear you say something about a pistol?

COP: I said it.

MRS. BAHR: *Starting to leave.* I'm a bystander.

COP: You're not going out until you tell me what guy lives here.

MRS. BAHR: *Pointing to* WAFER II. He does.

COP: Well, now . . .

MRS. NACH: I don't like a business with pistols.

COP: *To* MRS. NACH. Now confirm what she just said by telling me what guy lives here.

MRS. NACH: *Pointing to* WAFER. Him of course.

COP: You people are driving me to use my . . .

MRS. NACH: *Heading for door.* I was drinking my tea.

MRS. BAHR: *Also heading for door.* I'm taking a bath. *They run out.*

COP: Come back here!

WAFER: He's coming up with his son.

WAFER II: Who's coming up?

WAFER: Why, the man with the son who sees through a window.

COP: We'll get to the bottom of this.

WAFER II: There isn't anybody who doesn't know where he lives.

WAFER: *Transfixed, in a chant.* The cuckoo clock on the mantle knows where it lives.

WAFER II: *Likewise.* The ottoman against the sofa knows where it lives.

YOUNG WAFER: *Likewise.* The condom in the bureau drawer knows.

YOUNG WAFER II: The vaseline in the medicine cabinet knows. *The four men begin to stalk around the* COP *in a circle.*

WAFER II: All I know is that I know.

WAFER: What it is I know.

YOUNG WAFER II: Which no cop knows.

YOUNG WAFER: No neighbors know.

YOUNG WAFER II: And I know.

YOUNG WAFER: Which it's nobody else's business to know.

WAFER II: That I know.

WAFER: That's all I know.

WAFER: We'll never get to the botom.

COP: *Running to window, looking out.* They're coming up.

YOUNG WAFER: We got constitutional rights and the Bill of Rights.

YOUNG WAFER II: *To* COP. Get the hell out of our apartment.

COP: I'm standing here so help me with a pack of burglars.

WAFER: I never harmed a man in my life.

COP: Who are you?

WAFER: Somebody who lives here.

COP: Your name?

WAFER: Wafer.

WAFER II: Also Weiss.

COP: What's your profession?

WAFER: A pawnbroker.

WAFER II: Honest pawnbroker.

COP: Where are we?

ALL THE OTHERS: 777 Sedgewick Avenue . . . Bronx.

COP: *Still unsatisfied, to* WAFER II: Your name?

WAFER II: Wafer.

WAFER: Also Weiss.

COP: One of you is Wafer.

WAFER: Of course.

COP: Or the guy who called?

WAFER II: He could be Wafer.

COP: Who lives at . . .

ALL THE OTHERS: 777 Sedgewick Avenue . . . Bronx.

COP: How do you know he lives here?

YOUNG WAFER: He called and when you gave the bastard the address he said he lived here.

YOUNG WAFER II: And there isn't nobody who doesn't the hell know where he lives.

COP: But in *this* apartment?

WAFER: I know that I live here.

COP: *Taking out pistol, waving it, but finding himself still surrounded by the others who begin to close in.* Goddamnit, I'm standing here in this house making my report in this house at 777 Sedgewick Avenue, Bronx, and by the body of Jesus Christ I'm going ape, real shit ape, trying to see who's here and who's come in and who's coming in and whose property is WHOSE and who WHO and . . . *He springs away and stands with back to windows, unable to use gun.* I don't know where you guys come from and I wish you'd disappear like bugs but now you're here I got to make my report to the desk sergeant so if you guys'll just oblige me by giving me your names, not your names now, but your real names and who is what and what's the name, Wafer or Weiss, and who is whose father and who's whose son and where . . . *They are moving in again and he springs off into maze of furniture by door, the others tracking him.* you guys live and where you got a pawnshop and just what *kind* of a pawnshop since I been reading in the newspaper as well as reports at the station house about a pawnshop in the Bronx that they receive stolen goods in and the people live here in the west Bronx and I hear it's a man and his son or is it two men and a son who's supposed to be a son or two sons and a man who's supposed to be a man or I mean maybe two sons but then . . . *Standing back against door.* maybe you guys are straight and maybe then the other two downstairs who I hear on the stairs ain't straight and you guys are maybe detectives trying to head them off in disguise and so I'm in with you guys and so if you'll just move aside while I turn to try to attempt to move to turn the father the son to turn the suns to ah ah ah? let me ah ah ah get me ah ah ah in and here and out and ah ah ah . . . *With a cry he switches off light at door. Darkness. He opens door. Shots are heard.*

People are heard either falling or moving in room and on stairs out-side of door. Light comes on again by itself. COP *is alone in room, which is empty of people or furniture. Door is still open. Phone, on floor, rings.* COP *goes slowly to it, dazed.*

COP: *Slowly, into phone.* Hello? . . . Who? . . . You own the apart-ment? . . . Wafer and son? . . . Real name Weiss? . . . You're three blocks away? . . . And forgot your key? . . . Maybe it was robbed? . . . You're coming up? . . . I'll be here . . . *He puts down phone and goes into another room. Then* MRS. NACH *and* MRS. BAHR *come in, frightened.*

MRS. NACH: I heard noises.

MRS. BAHR: I got out of my bathtub.

MRS. NACH: This apartment's been vacant for months.

MRS. BAHR: No, it's the one down the hall.

MRS. NACH: Do people live here?

MRS. BAHR: A man and his son.

MRS. NACH: Where's the furniture?

MRS. BAHR: *Gasping.* A HEIST!

MRS. NACH: Where's an officer?

MRS. BAHR: Cops always come too late.

MRS. BAHR: They say cops are often part of those heists.

MRS. NACH: The owners of the apartment'll be dead when they see this.

MRS. BAHR: Such a nice old man with a son he says is his son.

MRS. NACH: I still say this is the vacant apartment.

MRS. BAHR: *Going to window, looking out.* I hear voices.

MRS. NACH: I said and I still say this is the vacant apartment.

MRS. BAHR: The voices are leaves on a tree up the block.

MRS. NACH: Leaves.

MRS. BAHR: *Whispering.* On the street.

MRS. NACH: I said and I'll still say this is the vacant apartment.

MRS. BAHR: *Picking up newspaper from floor, reading something that horrifies her.* Maybe it is. *The doorbell rings and a furious knocking is heard at the door.*

CURTAIN

The Death and Re-erection Of Dr. Franklin

BY EDUARDO GARCIA

THE DEATH AND RE-EREC-TION was originally produced by Lucille Talaco at the New York Theater Ensemble, 2 East 2nd Street, New York City, in August, 1969. The production was directed by Dorothy Dryden and featured the following actors:

PIANIST . . . . Marcus Grebler
ACTOR II . . . . Jerry Carter
ACTRESS . . . . Pamela Peacock
ACTOR I . . . . Robert Rosser
PLAYWRIGHT . . . . Ron Lane
DIRECTOR . . . . Herb Jarvis
PSYCHIATRIST . . . . Dennis Geisel
POLICEMAN . . . . John Black

Approximate playing time: 30 minutes

Stage is set for the rehearsal of a Shakespearean play. Platforms and ramps are scattered about the stage. A rehearsal throne is up center. A string of naked work lights hang down from ceiling. A piano is in its place in the pit. At rise, stage is dark. Noises are heard in back of the auditorium or off-stage. All characters come running unto the stage finding places to hide. Siren, police dogs, or mumbled voices of police are heard and then fade. A long pause.

PIANIST: They're gone.

ACTOR I *turns on his flashlight and scans the stage and the characters as they speak.*

ACTOR II: Pigs! Pigs!

ACTRESS: They didn't see us. We're free.

ACTOR I: We made it.

DIRECTOR: You can never be sure.

PIANIST: I can hear them.

PLAYRIGHT: Oh, no.

All freeze. Listen.

PIANIST: I can hear they're gone. No more bad vibrations—just harmony.

ACTOR II: *joyously.* They'll never come back.

ACTRESS: Never, Never, Never, Nev . . .

PLAYWRIGHT: Nevermore, quoth the crow.

DIRECTOR: QUIET! Where are we? You can't see where you are with all this noise.

ACTOR I: I found something.

He turns on the work lights. The lighting should be stark. All characters are dressed in semi-uniform. Colors should be institutional: cream and brown or grey and black.

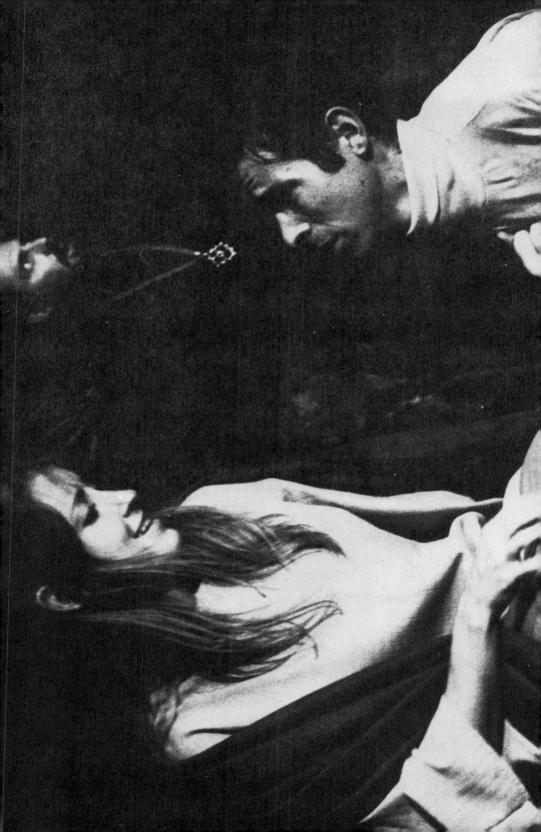

ACTOR II: *looking at audience*. Look!

ACTRESS: *screams*. What are they?

ACTOR I: There are millions of them. *Holding actress*. Will we be spared?

PLAYWRIGHT: It's a theatre.

ACTRESS: They're wooden. Chairs.

ACTOR I: They looked like people.

DIRECTOR: Feel it?

PLAYWRIGHT: What?

DIRECTOR: Feel the chairs? Feel the life in them?

PLAYWRIGHT: No flesh. Just wood and life!

ACTRESS: And soft seats.

PIANIST: And music. Joyous, boisterous strains—of sweetness.

ACTOR I: *bowing*. Strains—of applause.

DIRECTOR: *arms extended*. Thunderous applause.

ACTOR II: I must perform.

ACTRESS: *like a child*. Yes. Yes. I want to play. I want a play. Play a play.

ACTOR II: *singing*. I'll sing a song.

ACTRESS: *dancing.* I'll dance a dance.

PIANIST: Perform my concerto.

ACTOR I: *orating.* I'll orate an oration.

DIRECTOR: Unfold each moment.

PLAYWRIGHT: Write a scene.

DIRECTOR: But wait. Listen!

All freeze. There is no sound.

PLAYWRIGHT: No noise!

PIANIST: Silence. My enemy. KILL the silence.

ALL *except Director*: Kill the Silence—play a play. KILL THE SILENCE—PLAY A PLAY! Let's play a play. A play's a play to play and play.

DIRECTOR: Stop it! We must scout. Reconnoiter.

ACTOR I: Who knows what enemy may lurk behind those seats?

PLAYWRIGHT: What if we find a critic?

ACTRESS: Or in the wings, a terrible bird.

DIRECTOR: *to Actor II.* We must look around. *Points left.* You go that way.

ACTOR II: Yes, I'll go that way. *Exits right.*

DIRECTOR: And I . . . *Exits left. The other three peer out into the audience.*

ACTOR I: I see nothing.

ACTRESS: I feel they're looking at me.

PLAYWRIGHT: You feel it too? They must be looking.

ACTOR I: They have no eyes.

PLAYWRIGHT: No eyes, no ears, no mouth . . .

ACTRESS: No toe, no leg, no brow . . .

ACTOR I: No finger, no hand, no calf, no . . . *Caressing Actress.* thigh, no . . . thigh or leg . . .

PLAYWRIGHT: You see! You can only feel. Feel the warmth.

They stretch out their hands as if they are before a fireplace and enjoy the warmth.

PLAYRIGHT: The chairs are on fire. They're here to see us. To give us life.

ACTOR I: We better look around . . . I'll look in the thighs.

PLAYWRIGHT: A throne! Your majesty, your throne. Sit upon this throne and your servants shall do as you command.

Actress takes her place on throne while Playwright and Actor I kneel at her feet.

ACTRESS: Find the foes! Look high and low. Go now and look.

ACTOR I: Your ladyship gives us an awesome task. Our lives are in peril.

ACTRESS: Go or you'll have no lives.

The two men retreat from the "Queen" looking in and around platforms and moving out into the aisles.

PLAYWRIGHT: Nothing!

ACTOR I: No thing.

PLAYRIGHT: Not here.

ACTOR I: Not there.

PLAYWRIGHT: Nor here.

ACTOR I: There is nothing.

PLAYWRIGHT: Nothing. Oh, God why is there nothing. *Panic setting in.* There's so much nothing.

ACTOR I: We must report. *They scramble back to throne.*

PLAYWRIGHT: It's all nothing. There is nothing. No thing is nothing.

ACTOR I: There is no enemy. Wait! There is one place we did not look. We did not look low.

ACTRESS: Fool!

PLAYWRIGHT: Where? Where?

ACTRESS: Go and look. Look *now*.

ACTOR I: Here. *He lift her skirt. She screams to put it down running away from him, he chases her. Both are laughing all the while.* DIRECTOR *enters.*

DIRECTOR: What is this? Stop!

PLAYWRIGHT: We found nothing.

DIRECTOR: Did you find anything?

PLAYRIGHT: If only we could have found anything. But there was nothing.

ACTOR I: We found nothing.

ACTRESS: We looked and looked and then he looked . . . *Starts to lift her skirt and begins to giggle.* ACTOR I *starts chasing her again. They are interrupted as* ACTOR II *and* PIANIST *enter pushing a dolly loaded with costumes and all kinds of stage props: guns, knives, swords, etc.*

ACTOR II: Look what we found. *All rush to dolly and start pulling off clothes and grabbing props. They begin to dress themselves in wierd combinations (e.g., a nordic helmet with Roman toga etc.) of costumes and hats.*

PLAYWRIGHT: Life! They found life!

DIRECTOR: There was something. Thank God for something.

ACTRESS: Thank you, God, for something.

ACTOR I: There is everything. We have everything.

DIRECTOR: We must make a play.

PIANIST: Yes, and I shall create the mood. A symphony of drama; of tears; of laughter; and of joy. A shower of sounds to soothe the ear and excite the heart. *He begins again to play at his imaginary piano.*

ACTRESS: Let's play a play.

DIRECTOR: No, we must *make* a play.

ACTOR I: I'll act.

ACTOR II: I'll act, too.

PLAYWRIGHT: *at top of his voice.* I WILL MAKE A PLAY. I feel it. The Muses have called. I will write a play. Paper. Paper. Where is paper? *He starts looking through prop box.*

DIRECTOR: And I'll direct.

ACTOR I: I want to direct. I don't want to act.

DIRECTOR: Only I can direct.

ACTRESS: Why? I'd like him to direct.

PLAYWRIGHT: *discovers a scroll.* Paper! Yes. Paper, paper.

ACTOR II: I want only the best. What are your qualifications?

DIRECTOR: I saw a play once. I recall I *saw* a play.

ACTOR II: And you?

ACTOR I: No. No. I never saw a play. *Almost in tears.* God forgive me, but I never saw a play.

ACTRESS: Fool! *To* DIRECTOR. I want you. Only you can direct me.

DIRECTOR: *to* ACTOR I. Don't take it too hard, son. You can still act.

ACTOR I: *still near tears.* I never saw a play . . . *Starts to cheer up.* But I always wanted to be in one.

PLAYWRIGHT: Rotten society.

DIRECTOR: What?

PLAYWRIGHT: Rotten society! They all want to be *in* the play rather than see it.

DIRECTOR: That's why there is more feeling in the wood than in the flesh.

PIANIST: Where is my position?

DIRECTOR: Offstage, you idiot. No musicians on stage ever.

PIANIST: But I want to be on stage.

ACTRESS: You can't be in front of me, I'm the star.

ACTOR II: Go to your piano.

PIANIST: My what? Yes. My piano. I have it here. *Plays his imaginary piano again.*

ACTOR II: No, there is your piano. *Points to piano in the pit.* PIANIST *is stunned.*

PIANIST: It's a miracle. God is so good. *Almost in tears.* My soul—my life is renewed.

ACTRESS: It must be a miracle. I can hear you now.

DIRECTOR: There are no miracles.

ACTOR I: The king of sound! Take the king to his throne.

ALL *but the* DIRECTOR *form a processional line and lead the* PIANIST *to his piano in the pit. They sit him down. The piano is closed. He touches the closed piano with one finger. He hears the note and so do the rest. He begins to play with both hands and full force.* ALL *around piano sway with the music he is creating.*

PIANIST: Sweet heavenly sounds of superior beings. I'm enshrined in heaven.

DIRECTOR: We must play the play.

PIANIST: I'm playing. I'm playing.

DIRECTOR: *in panic.* WE HAVE NO PLAY! ALL *stop.*

PLAYWRIGHT: Yes, yes. I must write the play. *To* PIANIST. And you the music. Two gods of creation.

DIRECTOR: Men are not gods! Places. ALL *clamber on stage.*

ACTOR I: You've no pen.

PLAYWRIGHT: *distraught.* No pen! I have no pen! Great Muses forgive me. Do not ex-spirate me.

DIRECTOR: *hands extended over* PLAYWRIGHT. Let us all pray. Inspirate him. I mean, inspire him.

ALL: Inspire him. *A momentary church-like silence until:*

DIRECTOR: Enough of that. Find a pen.

PLAYWRIGHT: A pen. Yes. What is paper without pen? What is water without a sea? What is death without birth? That's what paper is without a pen.

ACTOR II: *having taken a feather out of the prop box.* Here is a pen.

PLAYWRIGHT: *writing.* First scene. There are two people . . .

DIRECTOR: Two people. *Two* people. You are no playright. There can never be a play about two people.

ACTOR II: It's more economical.

DIRECTOR: *as if reciting a litany.* There must be three. Three is the magic number. The triangle. The ETERNAL triangle. There must be three. Three sides to a shamrock. A trio of sounds . . .

ACTOR I: Three's a crowd.

DIRECTOR: *continuing.* Three's a crowd. Triangulation for effect. All movement must be triadic. B is to C to accent A. Three persons in one God. The Trinity. God Father in Three save us from two. There are three sides to every coin.

PLAYWRIGHT: It's a story about three people . . .

DIRECTOR: Threefold blessings on the Triumvirate Trinity; he has seen the light.

PLAYWRIGHT: There are two women and a man . . .

ACTOR II: I won't play a woman.

ACTOR I: I'm no transvestite.

PLAYWRIGHT: . . . Two men and a woman. They are in this house.

LIGHTS FADE *and* COME UP. *Actors assume positions on one of the movable platforms. The* DIRECTOR *is coaching them seriously.*

DIRECTOR: This is not a thesis play. This is life. Moment to moment. You cannot mouth words as if they mean nothing. Begin. Action.

ACTOR II *and* ACTRESS *say lines in same way a five-year old would read.*

ACTOR II: You act as if I don't care about you.

ACTRESS: You don't care about me and you know it.

ACTOR II: I've given you everything I have. I can't give you my blood.

ACTRESS: All you've given me is a baby I don't want.

ACTOR II: It's an expression of our love.

ACTRESS: You mean, your lust.

DIRECTOR: Cut! Please, please. You're not being Freudian enough. Give me the subtext. I want to *feel* the subtext. *Lines get closer to being "right" as* DIRECTOR *prods them with "subtext!"*

ACTOR II: You act as if I don't care about you.

ACTRESS: You don't care about me and you know it.

DIRECTOR: Subtext!

ACTOR II: You hate me don't you.

ACTRESS: No more than you hate me.

ACTOR II: I've given you everything I have. I can't give you my blood.

ACTRESS: All you've given me is a baby I don't want.

DIRECTOR: Subtext!

ACTOR II: I must retain my individuality. I never gave my mother anything.

ACTRESS: You're just like my father. This baby is mine.

DIRECTOR: Go on!

ACTOR II: It's an expression of our love.

ACTRESS: You mean, your lust.

DIRECTOR: Subtext!

ACTOR II: That was some night.

ACTRESS: It wasn't bad.

DIRECTOR: That's it. It's getting Oedipal now. Next scene. The two lovers meet. Live the subtext. *Platform is moved by actors to another part of the stage.*

ACTRESS: I swear, I don't know what I'm going to do.

ACTOR I: Try to bear up. As soon as the divorce comes through . . .

ACTRESS: You and your divorce. You keep hanging it over me like a fish for a seal. If you really loved me . . .

ACTOR I: How many times do I have to tell you . . .

ACTRESS: Love isn't all telling; it's showing too; it's feeling and giving feeling.

ACTOR I: I can't give what I don't have.

ACTRESS: I know, I know. I guess that's why I love you so much. You are honest with me. I know you love me but God I wish you would show it sometimes; outside of bed, I mean.

ACTOR I: You know what I always dreamed when I was a kid? I

always dreamed that when I looked at my wife she would melt. Just melt right there, and she would come to me and say how can you say you love me in so many different ways; just the way you look at me.

ACTRESS: Some people dream what they can't realize.

ACTOR I: And some realize that they can't dream.

DIRECTOR: No. No! No! Cut!

ACTRESS: I didn't say anything wrong.

PLAYWRIGHT: I thought she did well.

ACTOR II: I liked it too.

ACTOR I: I wasn't sure if she gave me enough . . .

DIRECTOR: Not her, you idiot. The music. It wasn't right. ALL *turn accusingly at the* PIANIST. *He begins to panic.*

PIANIST: That's a lie. A lie. I was reaching the souls of the audience.

DIRECTOR: Then it's a fault in the writing. Something's wrong.

PLAYWRIGHT: The play is perfect.

ACTOR II: I'm not sure I agree with that. The premise of . . .

PLAYWRIGHT: It's not the actor's job to agree or disagree.

ACTOR II: I would write it different myself.

PLAYWRIGHT: I have the right to write it as I want to write it.

DIRECTOR: If Joyce wanted to write an autobiographical play he would have . . .

ACTOR I: And if Shakespeare wanted to write a play about Rosencrantz and Guildenstern . . . or was it Guildenstern and Rosencrantz??? . . .

PLAYWRIGHT: I write what I want to write. The critic doesn't tell me what to write or what not to write but only if what I have written was written well.

ACTRESS: But who knows what is well and what is sick?

DIRECTOR: A doctor.

PLAYWRIGHT: Yes, a doctor. We need a playwright doctor. Maybe he can cure this mess.

DIRECTOR: He'll use his own needle.

PLAYWRIGHT: Yes, yes he will. He can't use his own needle. No doctor. I don't want a doctor.

ACTOR II: *screams.* Don't talk about doctors. Don't talk about doctors, and hospitals, and white and more white . . . just don't talk . . .

ACTRESS: Dr. Franklin. *There is an electric silence. The* PIANIST *beats on his piano building in tempo and crescendo:*

PIANIST: Kill. Kill. KILL! K I L L ! ! !

ACTRESS: KILL DR. FRANKLIN!

ALL: *in total frenzy—quickly until drained.* KILL DR. FRANKLIN! *Very long pause.*

DIRECTOR: *regaining.* We're off subject. Back to the play.

ACTRESS: *fully regained. Like a child.* Yes, I want to play the play. It's fun.

DIRECTOR: We must go on. The play must out.

ACTOR II: Time is it's enemy.

DIRECTOR: Time for the crucial scene. *Platform is moved again.* Do it right. All must be right. Don't forget the triangles. Triangulation must conquer. Quiet on the set. Lights. Action.

ACTRESS: But we have no lights.

ACTOR I: There's only darkness.

ACTOR II: Terrible. Fearsome. Alone.

PLAYWRIGHT: Darkness, oh darkness enemy of the stage. Enemy of the play.

DIRECTOR: A theatre in the dark is a like a babe in the womb. Only potency. No life; only a yen for living.

ACTRESS: Worth even less to many.

PLAYWRIGHT: Where is God now? Why have you forsaken me? *Fiat lux in me. Fiat lux in servos suos.*

ACTOR II: Let me be God.

ACTOR I: *Zaps him with line.* YOU ARE GOD!

ACTOR II: I am GOD. I am creator. I create light. Light be created.

DIRECTOR: What do you mean you are God? You are not God.

ACTOR II: *pointing to* ACTOR I. He said I was.

ACTOR I: We need a creator.

DIRECTOR: We all create. Creation is societal. We are what we are. We must ALL create the light.

ALL *sit in semi-circle facing the audience. They look up into the ceiling and begin a series of incantations all on the word "light." They use different tones and notes and they speak singly then in duet and then in threes until in a final frenzy all are screaming the word in unison. Slowly the lights pulsate with their prayers. Lights of as many colors should begin to flood the stage as the naked work lights dim.*

PLAYWRIGHT: We did it.

ACTRESS: The Minister always said there was power in prayer.

ACTOR II: Wherever two or more are gathered in *my* name . . .

ACTOR I: You're not God anymore.

ACTOR II: Oh.

DIRECTOR: We created it. Our minds did it. We made light.

PLAYWRIGHT: Like true actors. We brought it to life. Like an audience gives life and meaning to a play in imagination; in prayer we brought forth light. *Prayer-Meeting atmosphere.*

ACTOR I: Because we believed.

DIRECTOR: We must believe. There is no hope if we don't believe in something. Let there never be nothing. God be the eternal something. Be. Be. God, please be or we are not.

PLAYWRIGHT: *breaking the mood.* Enough theology. Back to the play.

DIRECTOR: Do you have your knife?

ACTOR II: No, I forgot.

DIRECTOR: Get the knife. ACTOR II *goes to box and takes a knife. He puts it in his pocket.*

DIRECTOR: ACTION!

ACTOR II: This is a real comedy. Here we are, the three of us: husband, wife, and lover.

ACTRESS: The eternal triangle.

ACTOR II: Or Trinity if you prefer.

ACTOR I: I didn't think you would have the guts to show.

ACTOR II: It doesn't take guts to face a rat.

ACTRESS: You call him a "rat". And what are you? A mouse. That's what you are. You never had the guts to face up to anything in your whole life.

ACTOR II: I faced up to the fact that I loved you.

ACTRESS: Ha! Love. Come here honey, let's show him what it is to love. ACTRESS *moves over to* ACTOR I *and they embrace and begin a passionate kiss.* ACTOR II *goes up and pulls* ACTOR I *away.* ACTOR I *tumbles to floor.* ACTOR II *then grabs* ACTRESS *throws her to the floor behind* ACTOR II. *She can't be seen by audience.*

DIRECTOR: The triangle. Preserve the triangle. ACTRESS *slides into "open" position so that she is visible to the audience.*

ACTOR I: You'll pay for that.

ACTOR II: Don't come near me, you savage. ACTOR II *pulls out the knife.*

DIRECTOR: Cut! "Savage." What is this "savage"? You're not talking to an Indian.

ACTOR II: It's what the playwright said to say.

DIRECTOR: *to* PLAYWRIGHT. Where's your theatrical intuition? "Savage" means nothing. It's got to have guts. It's got to be center-oriented. It's got to hit the audience right in the viscera.

PLAYWRIGHT: Say, "bastard."

DIRECTOR: More.

PLAYWRIGHT: What more?

DIRECTOR: Throw in a few "goddams."

PLAYWRIGHT: So throw them in.

DIRECTOR: Places. Action.

ACTOR I: You'll pay for that.

ACTOR II: *pulls knife again.* Goddman you, don't come near me, you goddman bastard.

DIRECTOR: That's better.

ACTOR II: *pulls knife again.* Goddam you, don't come near me. Please.

ACTOR II: Stay back. I swear I'll kill you both. *His memory begins to come alive.* It's what you deserve. You've no right to take my life away. I want my life back. I want you back. You can't take her from me. Give her back. Come back, Mandy. I want you. I don't want to lose you again, Mandy. Please, Mandy, come back to me. I didn't mean it. I swear I didn't mean to kill him. Come back.

DIRECTOR: What's wrong?

PLAYWRIGHT: Those aren't my lines.

ACTOR II: *torn apart.* I'm sorry, Mandy. So very sorry.

ACTOR I: Come on, you're an actor. Play the play.

ACTRESS: *The child again.* I want to play the play.

ACTOR II: Yes. *Getting back.* Yes, I'll play the play.

DIRECTOR: Action.

ACTOR II: . . . You can't take her from me.

ACTOR I: I'm not taking anything away from you. She's coming of her own free will. She loves me; not you.

ACTRESS: I want HIM. Not you.

ACTOR II: Then I want my baby.

ACTRESS: *Your* baby? Who do you think you are?

DIRECTOR: Cut! You goddam stupid playwright. You idiot. Look what you've done. You had her pregnant in the scene before, and now she's supposed to have a babe in arms.

PLAYWRIGHT: I'm sorry. I wasn't thinking. *His memory begins to*

come alive. I haven't been able to think. I want to think. I can't.
think. It's enough to make you go . . .

DIRECTOR: Do something.

PLAYWRIGHT: Yes. Yes. Transition. Sweet transition. There must be
a transition. Ah ha, transition: FIVE MONTHS LATER!

DIRECTOR: Okay! That's good. Now you're finished. The play is ours
now.

PLAYWRIGHT: Wait. I wrote it.

DIRECTOR: You've finished it. It's mine now and theirs and the au-
dience's. You've served your usefulness. Get out.

PLAYWRIGHT: But I want to make sure it's done right.

DIRECTOR: You've no rights anymore. Get out of here. DIRECTOR *goes
over to get one of the guns out of the prop box.* GET OUT!

PLAYWRIGHT: *memory again.* Don't send me away. I don't want to
go. I want to be with you. I love you. *To* ALL I need you. You
need me. I don't want to go there. It's a terrible, ugly place. Please,
please don't send me there. Can't you see how I've tried to think
. . . that's all I do is think. I don't want to go. Please . . . please,
I beg you. *He has fallen on his knees begging* DIRECTOR.

ACTRESS: *touched.* He doesn't really have to go.

DIRECTOR: We need a baby. You be the baby.

PLAYWRIGHT: I don't want to be a baby. I want to be myself. Why
can't you let me be myself.

DIRECTOR: *pointing the gun in his face.* You be the baby or I'll kill you. *His memory begins to come alive.* I'll kill you just like I killed Him. You don't fool me. I killed him dead. If I can kill GOD then I can kill you. You hear that. I can kill you. I will . . .

PLAYWRIGHT: I'll be the baby. I always wanted to be a baby. To be loved; loved so much and sucked at a breast.

DIRECTOR: There's your baby.

ACTRESS: *caressing him; wooing him.* Hello, pretty baby. You're my baby. Such a pretty baby. PLAYWRIGHT *buries himself into her lap and bosom.*

DIRECTOR: The play must go on. Don't stop the play.

ACTOR II: Then I want my baby.

ACTRESS: Your baby? Who do you think you are? This is my baby. My own baby.

ACTOR I: It's our baby. We're going to keep it.

ACTOR II: I'll kill us all first. ACTOR II *goes after* ACTOR I. *A scuffle.* ACTOR II *is victor and is about to stab* ACTOR I *when* ACTRESS *screams out:*

ACTRESS: Stop. Don't kill him. *She is holding on to her baby tightly, causing him to contort and begin to panic for fear of being strangled.* I'll throw him out the window. You hear. You touch him and I'll throw this baby right out the window.

ACTOR II: *relaxing his hold.* Your own baby?

ACTRESS: I swear it, I will. *Her memory begins to come alive.* I'll do it. I'll just take him by the head here and drop him. Just like I did the last time. Just drop little Chris right out like I did before. And I'll watch him fall . . . Oh, God, GOD, why did you let me do it? Why did you let me throw my Chrissy out? PUNISH ME! Punish me. THROW DOWN lightning and thunder, oh please . . . I'm sorry Chrissy baby, so sorry . . . *She is lovingly caressing the* PLAYWRIGHT's *head as she finishes in quiet sobs.*

DIRECTOR: No, no, no. It all looks fake. It's not real enough. You've got to really feel it before you can communicate it. If you get too involved you can't communicate. Snap out of it. This is a play. It must show reality.

ACTOR II: How much more real can you get than life itself?

DIRECTOR: On stage, life is unreal and reality is only what is created in the imagination. Truth must be truth.

ACTOR I: But I am truth. This is truth and I'm here right now. I'm free. Free. FREE. I'll never go back.

DIRECTOR: But that's not theatrical.

ACTOR I: Then why live? *His memory begins to come alive.* Why must we live if life is unreal and the real is fantasy. Sex is fantasy is real is life is fantasy. Where do I go now? *At that moment we hear noises in the back of the auditorium.*

DR. FRANKLIN: Here they are, officers. *The* DOCTOR *begins to walk down the center aisle followed by two uniformed policemen.* Just what are you all doing? *He continues to walk down the aisle until he appears in the light.* ALL *are terror-stricken.*

PLAYWRIGHT: *barely able to gasp the words.* Dr. Franklin! *With these words* ACTORS I & II *and the* ACTRESS *turn into animals haunched for the final kill. Dr. Franklin climbs onto the stage.*

DR. FRANKLIN: You sure made a mess here. *Now there is but an instant before the explosion. It is caused by the shrill harpie-like scream:*

ACTRESS: KILL DR. FRANKLIN! *At that instant* ACTOR II *lunges at* DR. FRANKLIN *burying his knife into his gut. The* DOCTOR *tries to defend himself but he is too late. Meanwhile* ACTRESS & ACTOR I *have gone to the prop box.* ACTOR I *gets a knife and runs in for the kill. The* POLICEMEN *have taken out their guns.*

FIRST POLICEMAN: *to* ACTOR I. Hold it! ACTOR I *doesn't.* POLICEMAN *fires.* ACTOR I *falls.* ACTOR II *panics and starts to run up a ramp.*

SECOND POLICEMAN: HALT! ACTOR II *doesn't. He too is shot. The* ACTRESS *now has a gun in her hand and aims at* DR. FRANKLIN *who has fallen to the floor gasping for breath, thinking he is mortally wounded.* ACTRESS *points the gun. The* DIRECTOR, *forgetting the gun in his own hand, tries to make the* POLICEMAN *stop. The two* POLICEMEN *jump for cover shooting both the* ACTRESS & THE DIRECTOR *in self-defense.*

DIRECTOR: *falling.* It was only . . . a play . . . only . . . *The* PLAYWRIGHT *is frozen in panic.*

FIRST POLICEMAN: Don't move. *All the while, the* PIANIST *has been going wild at his piano. As the last body falls, his masterpiece is finished.*

SECOND POLICEMAN: *to pianist.* That goes for you too. *At that moment, we hear laughter from one of the corpses.*

DR. FRANKLIN: *Unbelieving* I'm alive. I'm not dead. I'm not dead. *He begins to play with one of the retractable knives.* They were only play knives. I'm not dead.

FIRST OFFICER: *Looking at the toys.* They looked real.

PLAYWRIGHT: I wrote a play. It was only a play. It wasn't funny at all.

DR. FRANKLIN: *still to* POLICEMEN. I really thought I was dead. For one second there I really thought I was dead . . .

PLAYWRIGHT: You changed the ending. I wrote a play, but . . . *Picks up scroll.* . . . You changed the ending. You see, it's all right here. SECOND OFFICER *takes the scroll.*

DR. FRANKLIN: So real. So incredible.

SECOND POLICEMAN: There's no writing on this paper.

DR. FRANKLIN: Of course not. These people live in fantasy.

FIRST POLICEMAN: *looking at the bodies.* Some fantasy!

PIANIST: Oh my god, what glory. What reality. What power. The blood was gushing; pouring over my hands—the keys. Red melody. The creation of all creations.

DR. FRANKLIN: Well, if it isn't Kelly.

PIANIST: So real. So very real. The blood gave life to the music.

DR. FRANKLIN: Yes, yes it was beautiful, Kelly.

PIANIST: Every note—so clear; so perfect.

PLAYWRIGHT: You changed the ending.

DR. FRANKLIN: I know, Clark. I'm sorry. But think how there will be more room at the hospital now and you'll have new friends.

PLAYWRIGHT: *talking to the body of the* DIRECTOR. They changed the ending. They changed the ending.

DR. FRANKLIN: *tries to console him.* It was only a play, Clark.

PLAYWRIGHT: *holding the hand of the* DIRECTOR *and looking at the bodies.* Only a play . . .

DR. FRANKLIN: *ready to leave with police.* I really thought I was dead. I mean . . .

CURTAIN

117 Off-Off-Broadway Theatres

EDITOR'S NOTE: *All theatres and addresses off-off-Broadway are sub-ject to fluctuation. Some may be out of business by the time this guide appears. Productions are often staged on a highly irregular basis. In those cases where more than one theatre group uses a par-ticular stage, both units are listed. It should also be noted that not all the so-called "theatres" that make up off-off-Broadway are con-ventional playhouses. Many are churches, school auditoriums, store fronts, lofts, warehouses, coffee shops. All theatres listed are located in Manhattan, unless otherwise indicated.*

1. Actor's Mobile Theatre, 2109 Broadway
2. Actor's Place At St. Luke's, 487 Hudson St.
3. Afro-American Theatre, 15 West 126th Street
4. Airline Theatre Wing, Madison Avenue Baptist Church, 31st Street & Madison Avenue
5. Alamo Playwrights Unit, 218 West 48th Street
6. All Souls Players, Unitarian Church of All Souls, Lexington Avenue at East 80th Street
7. Amas Repertory Theatre, 4 West 76th Street
8. AMDA Theatre, 150 Bleeker Street
9. American Mime Theatre, 192 3rd Avenue
10. American Place Theatre, 423 West 46th Street
11. American Stanislavski Center, 251 West 80th Street
12. American Theatre Lab, 219 West 19th Street
13. Assembly Theatre Workshop, 113 Jane Street
14. Bastiano's Studio, 14 Cooper Square
15. Bed-Stuy Theatre, 1407 Bedford Avenue, Brooklyn, N. Y.
16. Blackfriars Guild, 316 West 57th Street
17. Cabaret Theatre at Noon, St. Peter's Gate, 132 East 54th Street
18. Chelsea Theatre, Brooklyn Academy, 30 Lafayette Street, Brooklyn, N. Y.
19. Church of Holy Communion, 6th Avenue and 20th Street

20. Circle Theatre, 2307 Broadway
21. Clark Center for Performing Arts, 840 8th Avenue
22. The Company, Holy Family Auditorium, 315 East 47th Street
23. Courtyard Playhouse, 137A West 14th Street, 424 West 48th Street
24. CSC Repertory Theatre, 89 West 3rd Street
25. Cubiculo Theatre, 414 West 51st Street
26. Donnell Library Center Auditorium, 20 West 53rd Street
27. Dove Theatre Company, 346 West 20th Street
28. Down Stage Studio Theatre, 321 West 14th Street
29. Dramatis Personae, 114 West 14th Street
30. Duo Theatre Workshop, 522 East 12th Street
31. Drama Tree Players, 182 5th Avenue
32. East Village Theatre, 433 East 6th Street
33. Elbee Audio Players, 621 West End Avenue
34. Encore Studio, 2345 64th Street, Brooklyn, N. Y.
35. Equity Library Theatre, 310 Riverside Drive
36. Expression of Two Arts Theatre, 102 West 29th Street
37. Extension Theatre, 277 Park Avenue South
38. Fortune Theatre, 62 East 4th Street
39. Free Store Theatre, 14 Cooper Square
40. Friday Theatre, 241½ East 84th Street
41. Fulton Theatre Co., 441 West 26th Street
42. The Gallery Players, Brooklyn
43. Gotham Art Theatre, 455 West 43rd Street
44. Gracie Square Theatre, 334 East 79th Street
45. Grand Theatre, 70 Grand Street
46. 98 Greene Street Loft, 98 Greene Street
47. Greenwich House, 27 Barrow Street
48. Greenwich Mews Theatre, 141 West 13th Street
49. Harbor East Players, St. John's Church, Webster Avenue and Ocean Parkway, Brooklyn, N. Y.
50. Heights Players, 26 Willow Place, Brooklyn, N. Y.
51. Henry Street Playhouse, 466 Grand Street
52. Hudson Guild Theatre, 441 West 26th Street

53.   Intar, 508 West 53rd Street
54.   Judson Poets Theatre, 55 Washington Square South
55.   Kings Players, 118 8th Avenue, Brooklyn; 275 Clinton
56.   Lambs Club, 128 West 44th Street
57.   Library of Performing Arts, Lincoln Center
58.   Little Broadway Theatre, 27 East 20th Street
59.   Little Church Around The Corner, 11 East 29th Street
60.   La Mama Experimental Theatre, 74A East 4th Street
61.   Manhardt Theatre Foundation, 542 La Guardia Place
62.   Manhattan Theatre Club, 321 East 73rd Street
63.   The Mask, 125 Fifth Avenue
64.   Matrix Players, All Angels Church, 262 West 81st Street
65.   Memorial Presbyterian Church, 186 St. John's Place, Brooklyn
66.   Mercer Street Playhouse, Mercer Street (between Bleeker and
      West 3rd Street)
67.   Meri-Mini Players, 4 West 76th Street
68.   Mt. Olivet Church, 86th Street & West 12th Street, Brooklyn
69.   National Arts Club, 15 Gramercy Park
70.   Negro Ensemble Company, 133 2nd Avenue
71.   New Repertory Company, 236 East 47th Street
72.   New York League of Playwrights, 162 West 21st Street
73.   New York Shakespeare Festival, 425 Lafayette Street
74.   New York Theatre of the Americas, 427 West 59th Street
75.   New York Theater Ensemble, 2 East 2nd Street
76.   New Old Reliable Theatre, 231 East 3rd Street
77.   Omni Theatre Club, 145 West 18th Street
78.   Opposites Company, 141 Prince Street
79.   Pageant Players, 450 Broome Street
80.   Park Avenue Community Theatre, 593 Park Avenue
81.   Park Slope Cultural Center
82.   Performance Group, 33 Wooster Street
83.   Playbox, 94 St. Mark's Place
84.   Players Workshop, 83 East 4th Street
85.   Playwright's Unit, 83 East 4th Street
86.   Potbelly Theatre Workshop, 40 West 18th Street

87. The Pretenders Theatre, 106 East 16th Street
88. Public Theatre, 425 Lafayette Street
89. Riverside Church Theatre, 490 Riverside Drive
90. Riverside Theatre Workshop, St. Johns-in-the-Village, 218 West 11th Street
91. Roundabout Theatre, 307 West 26th Street
92. Saint Clements Space, 423 West 46th Street
93. Saint Peter's Gate, St. Peters Lutheran Church, 132 East 54th Street
94. Schreiber Studio, 241½ East 84th Street
95. Senior Dramatic Workshop, 154 West 57th Street
96. The Shade Company, 230 Canal Street
97. South Bronx Community Theatre
98. Spencer Memorial Church, 152 Remsen Street, Brooklyn
99. Stagelights Theatre Club, 218 West 48th Street
100. Stagelights Two, 125 West 22nd Street
101. Ten Penny Players, 799 Greenwich Street
102. Theatre Crossroads, 23 East 20th Street
103. Theatre for the Forgotten, 106 West End Avenue
104. Theatre Genesis, St. Mark's Church In-the-Bowery, 2nd Avenue and 10th Street
105. Theatre for the New City, 151 Bank Street
106. Theatre Projects Company, 161 West 22nd Street
107. Theatre Three, Sloane House, 356 West 34th Street
108. Theatre 23, 23 East 20th Street
109. Thirteenth Street, 50 West 13th Street
110. TPG, 548 LaGuardia Place
111. Triangle Theatre, Holy Trinity Church, 313 East 88th Street
112. Truck & Warehouse Theatre, 79 East 4th Street
113. University of the Streets, 130 East 7th Street
114. Urban Arts Corp., Church of Holy Communion, 26 West 20th Street
115. Washington Square Methodist Church, 133 West 4th Street
116. West Side Actors, 252 West 81st Street
117. Workshop of the Player's Art (WPA), 333 Bowery